WHAT THEY TAUGHT US

WHAT THEY TAUGHT US

How Maryknoll Missioners
Were Evangelized by the Poor

Edited by
Joseph A. Heim, M.M.

ORBIS BOOKS

Maryknoll, New York 10545

Founded in 1970, Orbis Books endeavors to publish works that enlighten the mind, nourish the spirit, and challenge the conscience. The publishing arm of the Maryknoll Fathers and Brothers, Orbis seeks to explore the global dimensions of the Christian faith and mission, to invite dialogue with diverse cultures and religious traditions, and to serve the cause of reconciliation and peace. The books published reflect the views of their authors and do not represent the official position of the Maryknoll Society. To learn more about Maryknoll and Orbis Books, please visit our website at www.maryknollsociety.org.

Published by Orbis Books, Maryknoll, New York 10545–0308.

Queries regarding rights and permissions should be addressed to: Orbis Books, P.O. Box 308, Maryknoll, New York 10545–0308.

Manufactured in the United States of America.
Manuscript editing and typesetting by Joan Weber Laflamme.

Scripture quotations are from *The New Jerusalem Bible*, published by Doubleday, a division of Random House, Inc. 1998.

Grateful acknowledgment also goes to the following: Fr. Joseph Healey, M.M., *What Language Does God Speak?* (Orbis Books, 1989); *Once Upon a Time in Africa* (Orbis Books, 2004); *African Stories: For Preachers and Teachers* (Paulines Publications Africa, 2005); and *Small Christian Communities: Capturing the New Moment* (Orbis Books, 2005); Fr. James H. Kroeger, M.M., *Living Mission* (Orbis Books and Claretian Publications, Philippines, 1994); *Becoming Local Church* (Claretian Publications, Philippines, 2003); *Once Upon a Time in Asia,* edited with Eugene F. Thalman, M.M. (Orbis Books, 2006); Donald F. Sybertz, M.M., and Joseph G. Healey, M.M., *Towards an African Narrative Theology* (Orbis Books, 1996).

Library of Congress Cataloging-in-Publication Data

What they taught us : how Maryknoll missioners were evangelized by the poor / Joseph A. Heim, editor.
   p. cm.
      ISBN 978-1-57075-818-8 (pbk.)
  1. Catholic Foreign Mission Society of America—Missions. 2. Church work with the poor—Catholic Church. I. Heim, Joseph A., Rev.
   BV2300.C35W43 2009
   266'.2—dc22

                                       2008054872

For Victoriano Montes

Contents

Foreword

A funny thing happened on the way to the missions.

Armed with my seminary notes and skills and oozing righteousness, I went to the missions prepared to give but not to receive, to teach but not to learn. I soon discovered, to my great chagrin, that mission was a two-way street.

The people on the margins of political, economic, social, and sad to say, religious systems are the people we serve. What they lack in formal education and sophisticated eloquence they more than surpass by living near (or in) great violence and dramatic poverty.

In short, they live in a gospel or New Testament world, and so they evangelize us as we evangelize them. Mission goes both ways.

Joe Heim has done all of us a great service.

Most missioners are rich in these experiences, but these treasures are known only to the missioners themselves.

For these treasures to become yours, dear reader, it was necessary for Joe to contact, re-contact, implore, and implore again the missioners (very busy people!) to tell their stories. In the end, it was easier for us to respond to Joe than to keep coming up with excuses or putting him off. Thanks to Joe, you will meet these missioners and through them the wonderful people they have encountered. The missioners' treasure will become your gospel treasure.

Mission is to go to a no-place, to serve God's no-bodies, and, in the eyes of the world, to accomplish no-thing. Yet, in doing this we realize we are at the heart of what time, meaning, and history are all about.

Fr. John J. Walsh, M.M.
(from New York City)
Japan, the United States

Preface

How often have you read a scriptural text, read it again and again, and then, one day, like a shot out of the blue, something strikes you about those words? I was waiting for our community mass to begin a few months ago when, looking over the readings for that day, I read Matthew 11:25–26. "At that time Jesus exclaimed, 'I bless you, Father, Lord of heaven and earth, for hiding these things from the learned and the clever and revealing them to the little children. Yes, Father, for that is what it pleased you to do.'" If God has hidden things from the wise and the intelligent and revealed them to "the little ones," then it would be very smart of us to listen to them, the poor, those society has rejected. Whatever other mistakes we may have made as missioners, I think, for the most part, Maryknoll missioners have listened to the people of God and learned an immense amount of wisdom from them.

While I have had a firm personal belief that the world doesn't need another book, at the same time it seems important to share with fellow Christians some of the wisdom that we learned in our missioner years. That is why I wrote to fellow missioners, those still in the field and those who have retired from their labors, and asked them to share what they have learned from the people they went to serve.

I have dedicated this book to Victoriano Montes, our neighbor in Independencia III, a *barrio* in Barinas, Venezuela. Victoriano was not only a neighbor but also was my friend and a superb teacher. He was born about 1914 in the state of Merida, a mountainous area in the western section of Venezuela. In 1932, when their first son nearly died at six months of age because of a bronchial problem, Victoriano and his wife, Julia, gathered all their possessions together, loaded them on two mules, and began their eight-day trek down to the hot plains of Barinas. While they worked there as sharecroppers, they began to put together a small herd of cattle. One child after another arrived. Their daughter Pilar told me how her parents would take turns going to mass every other Sunday. One week Victoriano would lead half of the family on the two-hour walk to the nearest church, leaving the others with his wife. The next week would be Julia's turn, and Victoriano would stay with the other children. Each Sunday before returning home they would be treated to a breakfast of coffee and an *arepa* made of cornmeal and filled with cheese or ground meat. Served hot, the *arepa* is standard breakfast fare in Venezuela.

As the family increased in number, so did the herd of cattle, eventually reaching two hundred head, a result of hard work and a sharp eye for selecting animals. Then tragedy struck. When a neighbor threw a container of insecticide into a ravine, the poison seeped into the ground, contaminating the water supply to the Montes farm. In less than two weeks the entire herd died, and Victoriano and Julia, left with nothing but debt, had to return to sharecropping.

As their children grew to adulthood and moved to the city, the Montes remained on their small farm. It was there that I first met them in 1986, when I accompanied their son Felix, a neighbor of ours, as he brought them a supply of food. Their house was made of upright slats that kept out only the larger animals. It had a thatched roof, a dirt floor, and no running water. Later their children got together and purchased them a little house next to ours. Everyone referred to them simply as *Los Abuelos*, the grandparents. Every evening we could see ten to twelve of their children, grandchildren, and even great-grandchildren sitting in front of the house and chatting until the sun went down and the mosquitoes began to arrive.

Victoriano was more active than his wife, who was crippled with arthritis. He took part in every neighborhood

Generations of a family—Caracas, Venezuela

activity, helping to haul cement for the construction of the parish hall and enlisting catechists to teach the children. He had never gone to school, and so could not read or write, but he understood currency and was trusted by everyone to handle the community funds. Once when Fr. Tom Cronin and I had to go overnight to Merida, we asked him to guard our house. When we returned the next day at noon, his wife was bringing him lunch. When we asked why he had not eaten at our house, he answered, "You had not given me permission." Naturally, we had not thought it necessary to give him permission, but such was the integrity of Victoriano.

There was a lot of excitement in Venezuela around that time as many believed that the Blessed Mother had appeared to a woman in the state of Aragua, about a six-hour drive from Barinas. Many people were making pilgrimages to see The Miracle, as it was called. When Fr. Tom and I were talking with a few of the catechists one day, one asked if we were going to see The Miracle. At that very moment *El Abuelo* walked by in front of our house with his ragged pants, shredded cloth sandals on his feet, and a weather-beaten old straw hat on top of his head. Fr. Tom pointed to him and said, "Why should I drive six hours to see a miracle when there is one passing by right now?"

El Abuelo wept openly when Fr. Tom had to leave Venezuela because of ill health. Two years later Victoriano went to the Lord himself in the same quiet way that he had lived his entire life. This is why I am dedicating this book to Victoriano, to his wife, Julia, and to all the thousands of other people who, with no idea of how much they were affecting us, were such inspirations.

Many of us suspect that the Lord actually has a sense of humor. What else would have inspired the creation of an ostrich, a hippopotamus, or a monkey? For the missioner, a fairly concrete proof of God's humorous side is the experience that we who went out to preach and to teach would actually be taught by the very people whom we were sup-posed to instruct! And they would not only teach us local customs—how to make a thatched hut or what plants to use to treat hepatitis—but they would teach us about life and faith, and they would do it not from a pulpit but with their own lives. Nor would they have any idea that we were either impressed or astounded at their wisdom. In nearly every case these people had little or no formal education. It is not that the educated people were not helpful, only that the deepest wisdom invariably came from the "little ones." As St. Paul wrote in his first letter to the community at Corinth, "God chose those who by human standards are fools to shame the wise; he chose those who by human standards are weak to shame the strong, those who by hu-man standards are common and contemptible—indeed those who count for nothing—to reduce to nothing all those who do count for something, so that no human being might feel boastful before God" (1 Corinthians 1:27–29).

I am very grateful to the good Lord for what I learned in my thirty-five years in Venezuela. I also want to thank my fellow missioners—priests, brothers, sisters, and lay—who responded to my request to share their experiences of learn-ing from the poor around the world.

I also want to thank my niece Kate Campbell Heim, a freelance writer in Philadelphia, for her encouragement, suggestions, gentle criticisms, and proofreading of this manuscript. To her goes much of the credit for this publi-cation. (JAH)

Introduction

Perhaps the best way to begin this reflection is with a parable. It seems there was a bishop whose diocese served many islands in the South Pacific. One day as he was visiting various parishes, he came across an island that he had never seen before, so he had the captain sail over that way and, lowering a dinghy, he went ashore. There he found three fishermen who recognized his religious garb and greeted him. They told him that some twenty years before a missioner had visited them and taught them a prayer, but they had forgotten how it went. They did remember that the missioner told them that God was three. Since they could not remember the prayer he taught them, every day before going fishing they would pray, "You are three, we are three. Have mercy on us."

The bishop thought to himself, "We have a lot of work to do here," so he spent the rest of the morning teaching them the Lord's Prayer.

A few years later the bishop again found himself near that island and decided to stop and visit the fishermen. As his ship drew near, he saw the three men coming toward him, walking on the waters! As they came up to the ship, one of them shouted, "Your Excellency, we have forgotten that prayer you taught us. Would you teach us again how to pray?"

To which the bishop responded, "When you pray, say, 'You are three, we are three. Have mercy on us.'"

Celibacy

I am not aware of any statistics drawn from polls but I would suspect that most Roman Catholic priests would not have chosen celibacy for itself. Most of us probably accepted it as something we had to agree to if we wanted to be ordained. I never really gave any thought to its meaning. Then one day a very wealthy man and a practicing Catholic confided to me that he felt he was becoming too close to his secretary. Although he had not *done* anything, in his fantasies he imagined setting her up in an apartment, something he could easily do. Then he said, "But, I figured if you guys could live without a wife, I could live with just one." For the first time in my life I saw the prophetic value of celibacy: a sign to the world of the power of God's grace. There is only one way that we can be faithful to the vow of celibacy and yet be a caring and loving human being, and that is because of the grace of God. (JAH)

Children

And a little child shall lead them. (Isaiah 11:6)

In Nairobi traffic little children move in and out of the cars and trucks, begging. One little girl, no more than five or six, had a little brother tied on her back, and she looked to me for help. She had magnificent eyes, and I certainly would have given her whatever I had. Finding my pocket empty, I howled, "EEEE! Bahati mbaya, sina pesa!" (Oh, bad luck, I have no money!) "Siyo mbaya, Padri. Ni bahati, tu!" (It's not *bad*, Padre, it's just *luck*!) And she smiled the most forgiving and loving smile I had seen in a while. And I learned a lot from her . . . like never, ever to complain.

Fr. Thomas P. McDonnell, M.M.
(from Brooklyn, New York)
Tanzania and the United States

One day we were walking through a poor section of Lima. We came to the one-room house we were looking for and were invited in. As we came in the door a little boy greeted us. He had a small package of Oreo-like cookies. We were three, two women and myself. The boy carefully took cookies from his treasure and gave one to each of the women. Then he looked at me and looked at his package. One cookie was left, which he removed and carefully separated the layered delicacy and gave me half, keeping the other half for himself. For a moment I enjoyed the taste of chocolate, but for a lifetime I have enjoyed the memory of a little boy's generosity.

Bro. Martin J. Shea, M.M.
(from Springfield, Massachusetts)
Guatemala, Peru, and the United States

A schoolgirl tending her little brother—Tanzania

And, here is a sign for you: you will find a baby wrapped in swaddling clothes and lying in a manger. (Luke 2:12)

Sometimes it is an individual and sometimes it is a community that teaches us something about life and faith. Fr. Edward V. Davis, M.M., from Brooklyn, has worked in Tanzania and the United States. He shares the following experience from his early days in Tanzania.

A Christmas play, presented by the youth of our parish before the midnight mass, has become a tradition in many parishes of Africa. When I arrived a bit late at the church to watch the play, I found it crowded with people inside and many people standing outside. I thought to myself, No room in the inn tonight. Electricity had not come to Mwamapalala, and the church had only a few strategically placed kerosene lamps that failed miserably to light the church. The actors, in partial darkness, did not display any less enthusiasm nor did the audience show any inconvenience viewing the showy production. Everyone was enjoying and learning from the story unfolding in the sanctuary of the church.

As I squeezed through the crowd and found a standing place at the rear of the church, the angel Gabriel was making his way across the sanctuary and greeting a young lady, "Salaam, Maria. Umejaa neema, Bwana yu nawe." The angel's words to the virgin mother of Jesus were strong and reverent, and Mary's response was humble and obedient, "I am the servant girl of the Lord. Let it be done as you say." From her kneeling position Mary reached out—it was difficult in the dark to see what she was doing at first. She was reaching for a pole. She used the pole to pull herself to a standing position. And she did it quite clumsily. With the pole tucked under her arm to use as a crutch, she hobbled off the stage. The narrator began to tell us that Mary was preparing to visit her cousin, Elizabeth, in the hill country.

That should be an interesting trip for a girl with only one leg, I thought to myself.

Yes, I recognized the girl with the disability. She was a very sweet and good young lady from the village. She had been born with one leg substantially shorter than the other. Her disability did not prevent her from doing all the work that falls to the village women. She was very faithful in coming to church and participating in the youth activities of the parish.

Her crutch was a pole made from the branch of a tree. When she walked, she used the pole to do the work of the short leg that just hung from her frame, suspended above ground. Each step bent her body. When she rested and was just standing, the pole would be in one hand while the other hand rested on the thigh of her good leg. Even at rest she was partly doubled over.

I watched the Blessed Virgin Mary in the Christmas play bending in half as she walked to Elizabeth and then to Bethlehem, and I saw her awkwardness in holding the baby Jesus, embracing him with one arm and holding her crutch in the other. I watched how long it took her to stand and to welcome the kings who came to worship the newborn king. And all the while I kept thinking how really stupid it was to choose this girl for this part in the Christmas play. Don't they have any sense? Don't they understand how it was? My mild annoyance was growing into anger. I did not want to embarrass the girl, but the youth of the parish would have to be corrected. If they want to do a Christmas play, it has to be done right. It has to be perfect!

Then I started looking at the faces around me reflected in the flickering light of the kerosene lamps. Slowly I realized that I was the only one in that crowded church who was upset. Everyone else was absorbed in what was being said and what was taking place on stage. In the faces of the people the peace that the angel had proclaimed in his "Glory to God and peace on earth" was visible. All around me were people who were rejoicing in the good news that the Savior had been born for them and that Jesus had come to them as they are, as human, in their condition of being crippled and clumsy, being weak and powerless, being poor, being uneducated, being imperfect, just like Mary, his mother, was in the play.

I have not yet absorbed completely the lesson that the Africans taught me that night and that they continue to teach me so many times in so many different ways. They understand the meaning of the incarnation much better than I do. I still expect to find God in perfection. But there is so little perfection in my life and in my world, so little perfection in my life personally, in my community, in the work that I do, and in the people for whom I do the work. The Africans have been blessed indeed to recognize that God comes to us in the condition in which he finds us—in our crippledness, in our brokenness, in our clumsiness, in our slowness, in our failures. No doubt that is why they meet God much more often than I do. They can find God everywhere—in everyone and in every circumstance. Every minute of the twenty-three years that I have spent in Africa and every effort that I have made on behalf of the people here were repaid, many times over, that Christmas before the midnight mass in Mwamapalala. That night the Africans taught me that when the Word was made flesh, he delighted to rest in the arms of a mother with a short leg who bent in two when she walked. God wanted us to understand that Jesus was "God with us" right now. God is not waiting until we shall be perfect. (EVD)

Communists

Whoever is not against you is for you. (Luke 9:50)

Growing up in the 1950s and 1960s in what can only be termed an anti-communist era, I was very wary of communists in the slums of Venezuela. What were they *really* up to in their health and literacy programs, their food packages? We worked with them on community projects but always with a watchful eye. Then, in Barinas in 1986, I began to work with Fr. Tom Cronin. As it happened, we both needed to consult a lung specialist. Everyone said that the best one in the city was Dr. Edgar Rubio. We were advised, however, that Dr. Rubio was not only the head of the Communist Party in the state but also an atheist. That was not a major concern for us as we were looking for medical attention, not politics. And there was in fact no reason to worry. Rubio is a very quiet man and thoroughly professional. Except for the party literature in his waiting room, there was no evidence of his political beliefs. His receptionists told us that he didn't charge 60 percent of his patients and that included Fr. Tom and myself! When we told him that we could pay, his response was, "That's all right. You are helping my people." Dr. Rubio drove a twenty-year-old Ford that was so rusty that the original color was a mystery. He lived in a ground-floor apartment of a government housing project.

When we helped a group of women who were setting up a tapestry cooperative and were able to arrange for considerable sales in the United States, a fellow missioner criticized us and said that we were merely helping to create more dependency on North America. When I brought that query to Dr. Rubio he answered, "Anything that you can do to help people help themselves and put food on the table is good. Keep it up." In the strange workings of God's ways, one of the finest examples of justice and deep commitment that we found in Venezuela belonged to a group that would generally inspire fear and suspicion in us. (JAH)

Community

Fr. Ronald J. Potter, M.M., who passed away in 2004, had worked for many years in Guatemala. He once told of an experience while shopping in the open market of Guatemala City. He needed a large quantity of oranges for a celebration at the center house. As he walked through the marketplace, he saw an elderly woman sitting next to a crate of oranges. He asked the cost, and the seller told him the price for a single one or for a dozen. When he asked how much for the entire crate, she was taken aback and said that she couldn't sell the entire crate to him. Astounded that she would refuse to make such a sale, he asked the reason. She replied, "If I sold them all to you, I would have nothing else to sell. Then I would have no reason to stay here and meet my friends. This is the only chance I have to talk with them." Human relations were more important to her than commerce. (JAH)

While compiling material for this book I received an email from a friend in Venezuela. It so impressed me that I include it here.

In at least one African tribe there is a custom for a woman who becomes pregnant. She goes off to a separate place with other women and they wait until a song begins to come forth for the new child. They sing the song that day and on the day of birth. The entire tribe learns the song and sings it at every special occasion in the person's life, for example, at the coming of age ceremony, at the person's marriage, and again at his or her funeral. But there is another time when the community comes together to sing that song, and that is if the person has committed some crime or offended the community in some way. The person is put in the center of the group, and the tribe sings his or her song. It is

Women selling produce at the market—Guatemala

your song; you *are* one of us; you are our brother/sister always, and we sing to you. (JAH)

It was early morning on my first day in Irian Jaya. I was trying to get settled in my new home when an old Asmat fellow walked in without knocking and made himself comfortable in one of the chairs.

My previous experience in Indonesia taught me never to go straight to the point with people. We talked a long time, but when the old gentleman gave me no clues as to why he had come, I went back to my work, figuring he would catch on and disappear. He didn't.

I felt uncomfortable having him sitting there, so I came back and blurted out, "Is there something you want?" "No," he answered as he calmly stretched himself out on the short couch. Mildly irritated, I said, "Hey, look, if you don't want anything, why are you here?" This ex-headhunter, who was to become one of my dearest friends and mentors, looked puzzled and replied simply, "Because you are alone."

Fr. Vincent P. Cole, M.M.
(from Detroit, Michigan)
Indonesia

Conversion

He wants everyone to be saved and reach full knowledge of the truth. (Timothy 2:4)

One of the major teachings of scripture is that we are all made in the image and likeness of God. This tells us something not only about who we are, but also about who we can become. This is something that prisoners often find difficult to believe. Many inmates believe not only that they have *done* something wrong, but that they *are* something wrong. Few believe in their potential to become like God.

But one prisoner, Joel, taught me that we should never despair of God's grace and the capacity for a prisoner to change and realize his potential.

Joel was in a gang fight during which someone was killed. Joel was fourteen at the time, and one of the youngest of the gang members. He was therefore picked to take the blame, was arrested, charged, and found guilty of murder. He was sentenced to thirty years in prison.

I watched him over the years turn from a tough teenager into a kind and loving man. He showed me that most prisoners are ordinary people who made a terrible mistake or who have found themselves in situations with which they could not cope. After a few years of getting adjusted to prison life, Joel decided to study and get a degree and better himself. This he had to do mostly in his spare time, and mostly by self-study. He learned over the years how to take responsibility for his actions and how to be a responsible person. What he needed was the time and space to come to terms with who he was and who he had the potential to become. His becoming a Christian while in prison helped him in this regard. His reading of the Gospels reinforced the belief that we are all children of God. In prison he learned that grace has no boundaries. He saw God's mercy and power as always on offer and always powerful. He was able to slowly move from repentance to redemption.

Joel served twenty-two years of his sentence before being released on good behavior. He has since married and is working to support his family. The real clue to his new life lies in his having found a treasure in himself that gave him the foundation for his life on release. That treasure was the realization that he truly was "worth more than many sparrows" because he was made in the image and likeness of God.

This is something I had known in my head, but Joel helped me see it in my heart.

Sean P. Burke, M.M.
(from Cleveland, Ohio)
Hong Kong

Fr. Jesus Gazo is a Spanish Jesuit working in Venezuela. When he was chaplain in a city jail, one that was used for political prisoners, he got to know one young man who claimed to be an atheist. He didn't believe in any of "that stuff." They had many lively discussions, but the prisoner held firmly to his communist teaching. Then one day the young man asked to see Fr. Jesus and inquired about instructions in the faith and baptism. This was quite a surprise, because this man had been so adamant in the past. Quite naturally, Fr. Jesus' first question was, "What has brought this about?" He knew that it was not a result of his intellectual arguments, because people are not usually convinced for intellectual reasons and certainly not by arguments.

The young man then told the story of a recent "interrogation" to which the police had subjected him as they tried to get the names of his friends in the Communist Party. *Interrogation* means only one thing in political prisons: torture. He said that in the most excruciating moments of the torture, when he thought that he could not endure any more, he felt the strength to continue and not reveal the names of his friends. In that moment, he said to himself, "This strength does not come from me; it must come from somewhere else; it must come from Someone else." And so, the first step in his journey of faith began in a torture chamber of a Caracas jail and continued to baptism and total incorporation in the Christian life. (JAH)

Crazy

She was about sixteen years old and rather severely retarded. It was evident from her clothes and personal hygiene that her mother did not take very good care of her. For the most part she spent her time ambling around the *barrio* in Barinas, Venezuela, and never really caused any trouble. One day a group of women were gathered in front of one of their homes, and the young woman walked toward them. One of the women said, "Oh, here comes the crazy one." With that our young friend, sticking her nose in the air in defiance, walked away remarking, "Crazy is the person who calls someone else 'crazy.'" (JAH)

Faroque, probably schizophrenic, wanders the streets of Bagherhat in Bangladesh dressed in rags. He can speak English—when he speaks at all. Periodically, he evades the guard at the gate of St. Paul's Hospital and looks for me in the room where I give injections. He always grabs my hand, saying, "My friend, take me to America." Hand in hand we walk back to the gate, and I say, once again, "I can't do that right now." But one day Faroque appeared, trembling and covered with mud, with a deep cut over his eye. I cleaned him up, cared for his cut, and gave him a tetanus shot.

Later, Faroque looked for me, struggling against the guard who tried to shoo him out. Thrusting a plastic bag into my hand, Faroque said, "My friend, you helped me when the rickshaw hit me. A gift for you." In the sack was citrus fruit, some cookies, and an imported pear. We help hundreds each year from our Sick Poor Fund, yet this poor mentally disturbed man was the one who returned with his gift of thanks.

Sr. Bernadette Cordis Duggan, M.M.
(from Boston)
Philippines, Bangladesh, Cambodia,
and the United States

Culture Shock

In preparing for mission assignments overseas missioners are commonly warned to expect culture shock. As a young priest I went to work in the Philippines on assignment. I had prepared myself mentally for culture shock in my attempt to enter into a new culture and language. I was helped in this through an excellent language and cultural orientation program provided by Maryknoll.

My first local assignment was in Sigaboy, a very remote and poor area of Eastern Mindanao, a part of what was at the time the Prelature of Tagum, now the Diocese of Mati, Davao Oriental. While I had to adjust to many new things—linguistic, cultural, and physical—I never experienced the culture shock I expected. Perhaps this was because I had prepared in various ways.

I really experienced culture shock when, after three years of living and working in the Philippines, I returned home to the United States. It took me quite a while to readjust to my own culture and the social environment of the United States. In some ways I have never readjusted.

I began to analyze what had happened to me in the course of my three years in the Philippines and how I was changed. First of all, I was awed by the contrast in relative affluence. In the States people generally take for granted so much "stuff" that becomes essential to a contented life. Compared to the very poor people I had come to know in Sigaboy, as well as in other places in Philippines, it also appeared to me that many Americans, in spite of (perhaps in part because of) the relative affluence, were basically unhappy. This is manifested by the growing rate of divorce among married couples, the increasing incidence of young people resorting to drugs, the growing incidents of suicide among both adults and youth, the high number of "latchkey" children symbolic of a reduced personal contact between parents and children.

But in the Philippines I experienced people who, to a great extent, manifested greater happiness and contentment in life in spite of the fact that they had very little of this world's material goods and benefits. The Filipinos seemed to have a much greater appreciation for one another in terms of caring relationships. Again, though they had little in life materially, they seemed to be richer in terms of the quality of relationships. By their own example they manifested the priority of spiritual values over the materialist values that seem to pervade so much of American culture.

The Filipino people have taught me to value and appreciate much more profoundly the higher value of human relationships and the value of caring for others.

Fr. Thomas J. Marti, M.M.
(from Seattle, Washington)
Philippines and the United States

Death

The last of the enemies to be done away with is death.
(1 Corinthians 15:26)

Fr. Bill Donnelly, from Peoria, Illinois, went to his first mission, Guatemala, in September 1965. He was a witness, as were many of our missionaries in Guatemala, of more than one massacre of the indigenous population. The story that he shares here has to do with how a down-to-earth, faith-filled people deal with death, even the death of a child.

New to Guatemala and in my first parish assignment, I soon caught on to the fact that people would often ask for spiritual help and then take advantage of that to ask for some kind of material help. One night about supper time, some people came to the rectory in Chiantla, Huehuetenango, and asked me to give the sacrament of the sick or dying to a couple of young people who were very ill. They wanted me to go into the hills of the parish, which meant a long night drive. I said "OK," while wondering what else would be asked of me. Off we went, climbing up to ten thousand feet and then as far as my pickup would take us across the fields. We parked and started walking to a little adobe house.

As we entered I immediately saw a beautiful young girl of maybe seventeen years or so lying on a mat on the dirt floor and, on the other side of the room, her younger brother. I gave the sacrament to both of them. Then the parents asked me to take the girl, the sicker of the two, down to the hospital, which was farther down the line than Chiantla, a very long trip indeed. I responded that I really did not think the girl would survive the long ride. But the parents insisted, saying, "You are our only hope." What could I say but, "OK, let's go."

The people accompanying the family took the rustic door from the house and laid the girl on it. We carried her down to my waiting pickup and placed her between her father and myself in the only seat and began the journey. About halfway down the mountain the girl let out a gasp and died. I stopped the car. Her father cried, "My daughter!" I asked what we should do, and he said that we had to return to their home. As I gingerly turned the pickup around, the next thing this poor dirt farmer said was, "Thank God she received the sacrament."

As soon as the people on the mountain saw the vehicle returning they knew what had happened. By the time we arrived, things were well along in preparation for the night, which brought a long vigil in preparation for the girl's burial the next day according to Guatemalan law. (WJD)

Most of those who taught us were very poor. However, a rather well-to-do gentleman in my first parish, Newtown, Pennsylvania, taught me a vital lesson very soon after my ordination.

One Sunday afternoon I first met Maurice at the grade school football game where his grandsons played. He was a lapsed Catholic who went to mass once a year, on Christmas. And, as he explained, that was just to please his wife. He stood about five feet six inches and weighed well over two hundred pounds. We became good friends, and he invited me to have dinner at his house. His wife was an excellent cook, and he loved good food and fine wines. He would say: "I love to eat. I love life." Some months later his son called me and said that his father had been taken to the hospital with a heart attack. I jumped into my VW and raced to the emergency room, wondering what I was going to say to this sixty-seven-year-old man who had practically lost the faith.

As I arrived at the emergency room, still praying for some wisdom to know what to say, I found Maurice lying bare-chested on a gurney and sweating profusely. He was as pale as the sheet that covered him from the waist down. As I approached, he smiled and grabbed my hand with a strength that I will never forget and said to me: "Well, Father, this looks pretty serious. Here I am sixty-seven years old and with my weight a heart attack could be fatal. So I thought I should pray. But it has been so long since I prayed I couldn't think of any thing to say. Then it dawned on me that I know the Our Father, so I decided to say it. Then all of a sudden I realized what I was praying. I called God, Father. And it hit me that if God is my Father, then I don't have anything to worry about. I will just be going home. You can't imagine the peace that came over me. If I get out of this, I am going to tell other people what this experience has meant to me."

I was stopped in my tracks. I don't think I had ever witnessed the grace of God so immediately present. Maurice survived the attack and did what he had promised. He shared his experience with individuals and with any group that would listen to him. (JAH)

News travels fast in the poor areas. The Graterol family lived about twelve miles from the nearest town in the western mountains of Venezuela. A neighbor heard that a priest was in the area, and so the family sent for me. I followed the twisted path to the Graterol house, a tiny *ranchito* with a dirt floor and tin roof. Angustias was propped up with pillows in an old wooden chair. She quickly explained why she had sent for me, "No one in my family has ever died without going to confession. As you can see by the swelling in my feet, I have congestive heart failure and am dying, so I want to go to confession."

She could have had no idea what an impact it made on me that she was much more concerned about dying without confession than she was about dying! After hearing her confession I told her that we were having mass that evening and I would bring her communion. As the sun was setting, about thirty neighbors carrying candles and singing hymns accompanied me as I brought her the sacrament.

It is traditional for the priest to give a blessing after bringing communion, but the experience of her faith made such an impression on me that I said to her, "Señora Angustias, would you give us a blessing?" With that she stood up, stretched out her arms like the pope in Rome, made a few comments about the amount of alcohol that was being consumed in the area, and made a great sign of the cross over everyone.

I was not there when she died two weeks later, but I have no doubt that she went to her Maker with the same tranquility that she showed that evening when we brought her communion. I am also very sure that she could have not had the slightest notion of the impact that she made on the priest who ministered to her that evening. (JAH)

Ecumenism

Our orphanage in Tanzania housed abandoned babies who were HIV-positive or who had AIDS. A gracious Muslim woman would come regularly to help with the children. One day she asked me if I would accept her *sadaka* (charitable offering) as a gift for the children. She explained the Muslim custom of praying at a family shrine, commenting that when you asked for a favor such as healing for a loved one, a safe journey for a family member, and so on, it was customary to make a contribution for the poor. When the container was full it would be taken to the mosque and given as an offering for the poor. She loved our children and felt, as we did, that there were none poorer than these abandoned little ones. In her gracious humility she asked if it would be acceptable to bring her *sadaka* to the orphanage. We placed it on the altar and explained it to the workers and friends at the next mass. When we all agreed that such a prayerful offering would be used only for the children, they suggested a big party.

Fr. Thomas P. McDonnell, M.M.
(from Brooklyn, New York)
Tanzania and the United States

I had a fascinating conversation with a charming young lady. Although presently employed in Manila, she originates from Jolo, in the southern Philippines. In the course of our friendly chat she proudly told me how her name, Mary Ann, reflects her family, which is part Muslim and part Christian.

She narrated her background: "When my parents were choosing my name, it was my Muslim grandfather who insisted on Mary because of his admiration for Mary, the mother of Jesus the prophet. Furthermore, he urged that my second name be Ann in honor of Mary's mother. Thus, while acceding to my parents' decision that I would be baptized Christian, he believed that my Muslim heritage would not be lost because of the name he had chosen for me." She concluded her story, "I'm very happy that my own name symbolizes who I am—both Christian and Muslim."

Fr. James H. Kroeger, M.M.
(from Green Bay, Wisconsin)
(Excerpt from Fr. Kroeger's *Living Mission*,
p. 121)

*And, there are other sheep I have that are not of this fold.
(John 10:16)*

The parish of the Holy Cross was on the outskirts of Caracas in one of the poorest sections of the city. One Sunday after mass a parishioner asked me for a favor. Would I drive him to kilometer 9? It seemed like a rather strange request so I asked him what was at kilometer 9, and he said there was a woman there who cured. My antenna immediately went up. I asked myself if this could be witchcraft. "Why do you want to see a woman who cures at kilometer 9?" I asked. He then explained that his two-year-old son had not evacuated in three days, and he knew that this woman was known to be able to cure this type of condition. I asked him if he had taken the child to the hospital, and he said that after two days he had done that, but the doctor had said to take him home and if he was not better by the next day to bring him back. He knew that he would probably get the same reply today, so he wanted to have this woman cure his son.

Now, there is a vast gray area between black magic on one end and traditional healing or faith healing on the other, and, although I was sure this was not a question of the former, I was still concerned that I might be collaborating with some kind of witchcraft. Then I thought that if I had a son and had received the kind of treatment that the local hospital was famous for, I would use any means to have the child cured. So off we went.

We found the woman in question. She lived in a small mud house with a tin roof. As soon as she knew what the problem was, she immediately sent her daughter out to an orange tree to bring in some of its leaves. She put on water and proceeded to boil the leaves. Then she began to massage the baby's stomach with olive oil as she asked the father about the child's diet. Other members of the family joined in and offered their opinions. I realized this was becoming a community event. When the orange tea was ready, she cooled it so the child could sip it. Then she returned to massaging the stomach with olive oil and at one point made three signs of the cross on the abdomen. I was watching everything very carefully, and as she made the signs of the cross I thought to myself that a priest might do the same thing.

After about forty minutes the small boy broke some wind and everyone smiled; this was going to be a success. As she kept up the massaging and offering more tea, he broke more wind and now everyone was satisfied. After assuring the father that the boy would return to normal in a few hours and that he should not worry, she gave him some orange leaves to take home and make more tea. As we were leaving, the father asked how much he owed her. She said, "Ten *bolivares*." Ten *bolivares* at the exchange rate of that time was exactly two dollars and twenty cents. It had taken a full hour, the entire family was involved, and the only elements used were orange leaves and olive oil. (JAH)

I have often spoken about my 100-year-old Muslim friend and landlord, now deceased, Kashem Ali, and how he had once read the account in the Gospel of Matthew of Jesus' cry as he was dying on the cross. At Jesus' cry, *Eli, Eli, lama sabacthani*, Kashem commented, "He is calling Allah." Kashem realized that *Eli*, the Hebrew word for God, was the same as Allah in Arabic. He saw Jesus' faith in our mutual God. What a sharp reflection for a man then in his nineties.

One day he called me to his room. "I am dying," he said, "and I want to apologize to you for any ill I have done to you."

I was and still am astounded at this sincere confession from this Muslim. Could a Christian have done more?

Fr. Douglas F. Venne, M.M.
(from Milwaukee, Wisconsin)
Philippines and the Muslim community
in Bangladesh

When I am asked, "What are your thoughts on the Islamic religion?" I respond by talking about the faith of Muslims. I only know a little about Islam, but I am close to many Muslims. First, I need to say that the man who most influenced me to spend my life among my brother and sister Muslims was Blessed Charles de Foucauld. Though he scandalized others in his early life, he had the courage to travel to Morocco in the 1880s, when the fate of many foreigners was death. There he noticed how sincere the Muslims were in their prayer. Muslims praying five times a day certainly impressed de Foucauld. When he returned to France, he decided that he should look into his own faith. He found God again and never turned back.

I also witness the prayers of my neighbors five times a day. This does not mean that everyone prays, but most do. It is impressive. When I first went to Bangladesh some of my Christians companions complained about the noise coming from the amplifiers (simply called "mikes" in Bangladesh) five times a day. Indeed, some amplifiers were aimed at Christian enclaves. It took me a while to realize that the Muslims were praying to my God, not just irritating the population. I said to myself, "If they are called to prayer five times a day, so am I and so are all Christians."

A Muslim at prayer

(My breviary indicates Christian prayers for seven times each day, but we don't have official calls to remind us.)

When you stop to think about it, there are a billion Muslims in the world, spread out in all directions. Many respond to prayer five times daily, if not in the mosques, at least in their own homes. Some even pray in the streets or while riding buses or trains. An Arab astronaut did his prayers in space. Since he passed the sun every ninety minutes, he could not follow the traditional times so he prayed according to the time in Mecca.

Some think such prayers are pharisaical. A billion people? No, we have to accept their sincerity in prayer, as real as our praise of God who made us all. In the end I decided that the call to prayer from the Muslim minarets was meant for me too. When I hear the call, I say, "Our Father, thy kingdom come." Just those few words are enough. Yes, our common Father will bring us together if we pray and work for unity with others.

Fr. Douglas F. Venne
(from Milwaukee, Wisconsin)
Philippines and the Muslim community
in Bangladesh

Fr. Joseph G. Healey, M.M., from Baltimore, began his mission career in Africa. In the course of his work he began collecting wisdom stories and has published them in several books.

One day my pickup truck broke down on the road from Maswa to Bariadi in western Tanzania. After I had waited for half an hour, a big Coca-Cola truck came by and the driver, named Musa, kindly towed my vehicle to the next town. This was a not-uncommon occurrence of friendship and mutual help on our poor dirt roads.

While we drove into town I sat in his big cab and we talked about, of all things, religion. Musa was a Muslim who belonged to the Nyamwezi ethnic group. In commenting on the tensions between Christians and Muslims in Tanzania, he said, "There is only one God. God is like a large baobab tree with different branches that represent the different religions of Islam, Christianity, African religion, and so forth. These branches are part of the same family of God— so we should work together." Simply put, Musa gave me a wonderful African metaphor for world religions and inter-religious dialogue. (JGH)

Excerpt from *Once upon a Time in Africa,* p. 127

Eucharist

They have been with me now for three days and have nothing to eat. (Mark 8:2)

Fr. Paul D. Belliveau, M.M., from Brooklyn, worked in Guatemala and the Mesa Grande refugee camp in Honduras. His present assignment is in pastoral care at St. Teresa's Residence at Maryknoll, New York. He shares the following story from his experiences in the refugee camp in Honduras.

For the last two weeks there had been a food shortage in the camp. During normal times an eight-day ration of black beans, corn, and coffee was given to each family every Saturday morning. All the food came from San Pedro Sula in trucks and arrived at different intervals and then was stored in wooden buildings throughout the camp. For days the trucks did not arrive. It was the eleventh day since the people of Camp #6 had last received food, and many had not eaten anything for three days. So the Catholic women went from tent to tent in Camp #3 collecting corn. They made three hundred tortillas and took them to Camp #6 and gave them to the children. They saw the need of others. In spite of having little food themselves, they gave from their own need so that others could eat. They became eucharistic. I was amazed at these people who were evangelizing me and making the gospel become real. (PDB)

Sister Elizabeth V. Roach, M.M., from Pittsburgh, Pennsylvania, worked for many years in the missions of Bolivia and Peru. She has written several books, including *If I Am Found Worthy: The Life of William C. Kruegler, M.M.*, the story of a missioner who was assassinated in Bolivia in 1962. Sister Elizabeth spends her

Worship in a poor chapel—Santa Rita villages, Guatemala

retirement tending the library in the Rogers Building and volunteering with the Spanish-speaking prisoners at Sing Sing.

No place to sit down, no pews, no benches, but Christ was present. The chapel had only a thatched roof supported by saplings cut by the men of the community. One couple came carrying a table from their house for the altar. Someone else brought a chair so the priest could sit down to hear confessions. Another brought boiled water.

The people had walked a long way for the weekly eucharist. They stood on the rain-soaked mud floor all through the mass. Now the men were standing for a meeting with the priest.

Some women who had never learned to read but wanted to receive the sacraments had asked me to teach them the prayers. I taught them by rote, explaining one phrase a week. They had learned the Our Father and the Hail Mary. That day, with some hesitation, I asked, "Do you want to learn the Apostle's Creed?"

Maria, a frail young mother holding her baby in her arms, clasped her hands together as if in prayer. She said, "Oh, Sister, please, that is such a beautiful prayer and all my life I have wanted to learn it."

Maria deepened my faith that day. Unknown, unsung, unlettered, she proclaimed her faith like another Maria who once stood by the cross and is called blessed because she believed!

I've learned that for those who believe it is nothing at all to pick up their kitchen table and carry it a long way so that their community can have an altar when a priest comes to offer mass. (EVR)

Faith

If your faith is the size of a mustard seed, you will say to the mountain, "Move from here to there," and it will move; nothing will be impossible for you. (Matthew 17:20)

Fr. J. Lawrence Schanberger, M.M., from Baltimore, has worked in Chile, Venezuela (where he served as a regional superior), New York (as rector of the seminary), and Bangladesh. Health problems have forced this eighty-four-year-old missioner back from Bangladesh, but he continues in pastoral work in his original mission in Chile.

On May 21, 1960, at 4:00 a.m., a violent earthquake struck Talcahuano, Chile. That afternoon the naval base warned people that a tidal wave was on the way and that all people living in houses on the beach should immediately leave their homes and take to the hills. The pastor of the parish asked me to go and advise the people on the beach near the parish to leave their homes and quickly go up to the nearby hills.

To my amazement, a group of the people responded, "Before we go we want to take the statue of the Blessed Mother from our small chapel and have a procession on the beach." And so they did! Then they returned the statue to the chapel, closed their houses, and headed for the hills. Not long after, the tidal wave arrived and passed directly in front of their houses and kept going south where it swept into the town of Valdivia, destroying everything. (JLS)

Rev. Alphonse A. Schiavone, M.M., from Hartford, Connecticut, was first assigned to Africa and then worked in Colombia before being assigned to formation work in the United States. At eighty-six years of age he refuses to retire and works as a counselor in the Office of Society Personnel at Maryknoll, New York.

Veronica and Cecilia were two elderly women who were wards of the Kilulu mission in the Shinyanga diocese of Tanzania. They would come to clean the chapel and collect their three shillings to buy meat for the week.

They lived together in a little mud and branch hut at the edge of the mission property. Veronica was blind and Cecilia was a leper whose hands were just stubs.

Regularly each Saturday morning they came to the mission to do their chores. They arrived holding hands, singing and laughing. Cecilia led Veronica to the backless benches, gave her a rag, and guided her to the benches at the entrance of the chapel. Veronica felt her way, singing a song she made up as she went along. Cecilia went to the sacristy to sweep the concrete floor.

I returned about an hour later to give them their food money. The sacristy floor was swept clean, but I noticed some drops of blood on the floor behind Cecilia. I also noticed that the broom had not been used and Cecilia was hiding her hand behind her back. She had swept the floor with her hands. I scolded her and asked her why she had done such a thing. Her eyes filled with tears as she said, "God has been so good to me that I wanted to show how much I love him."

Fifty years later I was giving a homily on the visitation. As I spoke, for some strange reason, Cecilia came to mind. It was then that I realized she had been saying her Magnificat (Luke 1:46–55). (AAS)

And, Jesus said, "Woman, how great is your faith." (Matthew 15:28)

Lilia de Liendo was a member of our parish council in Holy Spirit Parish in Valencia, Venezuela. Lilia had her own business and was a hard-working and self-assured woman.

She told me one day that when her four-year-old son was playing with friends in a neighbor's yard he had gotten into a tool shed where he found a sickle and began to swing it back and forth. Before anyone realized that he had the instrument in his hand, he had severely cut his left eye. His mother rushed him to the local hospital where, fortunately, the best eye surgeon of Venezuela happened to be visiting. She ran to him, and when she explained what had happened, the doctor began to reprimand her for her negligence. She acknowledged, "Oh, yes, it is my fault, but you *will* operate on my son, won't you?" Instead of attending to the boy, the doctor continued to scold the mother, saying that since she was such a negligent mother, he didn't think he should help her.

The mother immediately replied, "Oh, yes, you are right, doctor. I am a terrible mother and don't deserve any help, but this is my son and you *will* operate on him, won't you?" The surgeon continued several more times in the same vein and the mother continued to accept his insults but begged him to operate. He finally did operate and saved the boy's eye.

As she related the event, I kept thinking how in any other circumstance she would never have allowed anyone to speak to her in that manner, but for the sake of her son, she accepted it all. This was the power of love. I reminded her of the Canaanite woman in the Gospel of Matthew (Matthew 15:21–28), the woman who continued to pursue Jesus, and how she had acted in the same way. It was also all because of her love for her child. (JAH)

Rev. William F. Mullan, M.M., from Brooklyn, has worked in both Guatemala and the United States. He is currently in Guatemala.

The elders of the village Rax Ik (Green Chiles) met me as I came in to the village after walking several hours, partly through the jungle. They asked me to begin my pastoral

Traditional dress and traditional prayer—Guatemala

visit by going with them to the source of the drinking water. It was a spring that came up from a deep hole and formed a pool of clean water. However, at this time of the year, it was drying up, and the people had to send buckets down into the hole to come up with water. The elders asked me to join them while they prayed with incense and candles. They gave me a candle to hold.

While we prayed, I looked up at the tree above us and I saw about eight howler monkeys looking down at us; it was their source of water also. We left the candles burning around the hole. The elders prayed for me with incense and took me into the small chapel where the people were waiting and we began mass. During the prayers of the faithful all the adults were given candles, and with the elders leading us we thanked God for the gift of the water, corn, and animals. We asked God to bless the gifts and also their children, who need these gifts for life.

There is no doubt in the Mayan people's minds and hearts that we depend absolutely on God's gifts of sun, earth, rain, seeds, and animals for life. I have learned that from being with them so often in prayer. I don't think many people in the United States kneel down and pray that there are tomatoes and potatoes in the supermarket before they go to shop, and hardly anyone thinks of God as the source of the food that we eat. (WFM)

Deborah Northern, originally from Warsaw, Virginia, is a former Maryknoll lay missioner. She joined Maryknoll in 1999 and worked first in Tanzania, teaching at a Catholic university until 2003, when she transferred to El Salvador, where she was part of an AIDS ministry doing preventive education.

Recently, I have become even more aware of what "blind faith" really means. One day I witnessed a blind man, carrying a white cane, approaching a very busy intersection. Without fear or hesitation, he entered the intersection as he blew loudly on a whistle, trusting that the buses and cars would let him cross safely, and they did. Even though I am able to see, I continually fear crossing this same intersection.

Another day, riding on the bus and looking out the window, I saw a sighted musician carrying his guitar. He was leading two blind musicians, who were holding their own instruments, through the congested and often uneven sidewalks downtown. The first blind musician had a hand on the shoulder of the guitarist, and the one behind had placed a hand on the first man's shoulder so both could follow in the path of their guide.

I began to reflect on my own faith. Did I have the kind of faith to follow God blindly, or would I hesitate out of fear? Also, would people have the confidence to follow in my footsteps?

When I was doing an internship in the Counseling Center at James Madison University, one of my mentors was blind due to diabetes. He would often ask me to escort him around campus, taking my elbow as he walked beside me. Unfortunately, I would sometimes forget he couldn't see and neglect to inform him about curbs and steps. It amazed me that he continued to trust me. From now on I try every day to have more trust and faith in God, even though I can't always see where God is leading me, and I try to be a more trustworthy leader to those entrusted to my care. (DN)

Family

A few months ago I was invited to have lunch in the home of a Mayan family. It was a small one-room building with bare wooden boards as walls, and the roof was made of palm leaves. The home had several wooden beds with mosquito nets hanging over each one. The floor was dirt, but everything was clean, including the floor. I was invited to sit at a small wooden table while the woman of the house began to make tortillas and heat beans and rice for my lunch. The man of the house sat on a small tree trunk that served as a chair. The young children, three girls dressed in the traditional clothes and a boy, smiled and answered my questions with delight. As I have observed so often, they seemed to be very happy and content to be in this family, with their parents who love them.

Very often when I am on vacation back home and visit a family with small children each child shows me his or her own stack of toys, which may have cost several hundred dollars. I looked around the simple house of this Mayan family and saw that there was not one thing that any of those children would claim to be their own; I didn't see a single toy. The only "extra" item in the house was a small radio that received only two stations.

From what I have seen and understand, I have concluded that for the Mayans the greatest success a man and woman can achieve in life is to form a family, to have children, and to be able to clothe and feed them and to teach them to be good people who respect God, nature, and the community.

Fr. William F. Mullan, M.M.
(from Brooklyn, New York)
Guatemala and the United States

Fr. Bill Mullan baptizes a baby

I was leading a workshop on self-esteem in a small, rural parish. I had prepared a handout that included several statements, and I asked the participants to decide whether or not these statements or situations would lead to higher self-esteem. The first statement read, "I can make decisions on my own." I asked the participants to raise their hands if they felt this statement reflected a sense of self-esteem. No one raised a hand. Thinking that they hadn't understood my Spanish, I tried again. Still, no response.

Finally, my co-presenter, a Salvadoran, repeated the question, but this time asked how many people felt this statement did *not* reflect a sense of self-esteem. Everyone raised a hand. Then he asked people to explain their response. In Salvadoran culture decisions are based on talking and consulting with family and friends. Only people without family or friends would have to make decisions on their own!

I was looking at the question from my own cultural perspective. I realized that I need to understand the cultural context of the people where I am working and not make assumptions from my own point of view. In retrospect, their point of view is valid and healthy. I can learn from the people of El Salvador new ways of looking at self-esteem and life!

Deborah Northern, MMAF
(from Warsaw, Virginia)
El Salvador

Forgiveness

And that is how my heavenly Father will deal with you unless you forgive your brother from your heart. (Matthew 18:35)

In August 1981 I went up from Guatemala City to San Mateo Ixtatan in Huehuetengo, a drive of about eight hours. I had been pastor there for six years before I was elected to be the regional superior for the Maryknoll Society in Central America, which required that I move down to Guatemala City. Fr. Ron Henessey, the former regional superior, then took my place in San Mateo parish. He had mailed me a copy of an article he had written describing the recent massacres of almost one thousand Mayan Chuj-speaking people in the different villages of the parish. At his request we sent the description to one of his sisters, a nun in the United States. She submitted it to several newspapers, and it was widely published.

Now I was returning to San Mateo to visit Ron and the people. I knew it would be a difficult visit and that Ron would be in danger from the military, who had to be very angry with him for sending out his report. These were also people I loved to be with and serve, and I had known many of those who had been massacred.

While I was standing outside the four-hundred-year-old church, I saw about twenty soldiers holding Israeli machine guns just across the road. They were standing there with chickens, pigs, horses, and several small radios around them. Ron had told me that they were selling what they had looted after the massacres. I stood there and for the first time in my life I began to have feelings of hatred.

Tumik, a Mayan woman of about sixty years, came over to me and said simply, "Father, they are our brothers. I would give them a glass of water if they asked." Tumik had become a member of the Catholic Church while I was pastor there. I turned away from the scene and with Tumik went into the church to concelebrate a mass with Ron for the dead and for the soldiers. Jesus does challenge us with "love your enemies"!

Fr. William F. Mullan, M.M.
(from Brooklyn, New York)
Guatemala and the United States

Fr. Ernest C. Lukaschek, M.M., from Brooklyn, was ordained in 1962 and has worked in Chile and the United States. He is currently the pastoral director of our center at Maryknoll in New York.

Rosa is a Mapuche woman living in the city of Santiago with her family. Like most of the Mapuches, the indigenous people of Chile, she was born and raised in the countryside. Her life in the southern part of Chile was not an easy one because of the climate, which is very cold and rainy during the winter, and poverty. It was made worse by an alcoholic father who quite often cursed and beat his family. In his old age—he was almost one hundred years old when he died—he became very sickly. Because of his drinking, he had also been long separated from his family.

However, Rosa could not forget that he was her father "no matter what," as she once told me. She went looking for him in southern Chile, found him, and brought him back to live with her and her family until he died. Because Jesus told us to forgive, she forgave her father and opened her heart and her home to him. (ECL)

Fr. Anselmo Cerro, a Venezuelan priest who worked with us in our parish in Valencia, told this story of when he was preaching one Sunday in a make-shift chapel on the bottom floor of a local school. In his sermon on the topic of

forgiveness he mentioned a case in which a man had abandoned his wife and six children to marry a younger woman.
Then, years later, when he became ill, the other woman
abandoned him, but his first wife took him back and nursed
him until his death.

No sooner had Fr. Cerro finished the story when a woman
in the congregation stood up and said, "That is what happened to me." And, proceeding to tell of her identical experience, she recounted how her children had all collaborated
in caring for their aged, returning father. (JAH)

In Bangladesh an owner who has more goats or cows
than needed will let a poor family care for one. When I
bought a goat, I asked Kangal and his wife, Khudeza, to care
for it. They were very eager to do it, so I placed the animal
with them. Later on, since my vacation to the United States
was near, I asked Kangal if I could see the goat. "It is with
my wife at her mother's place." I went there but she didn't
have it. The truth came out that they had sold it. I blew my
stack. Kangal and I were finished. He would get no more
special consideration despite his telling me that I was his
best friend.

Along came Kalu Mia. (It was Kalu, a nineteen-year-old
day laborer, who had introduced me to village life when he
convinced his employer to let me work in the fields.) Kalu
knew the story of my goat, and he brought his friend Kangal
and me together. He sat on the ground between us. On his
left was Kangal, who hung his head down, and I, fuming,
sat on Kalu's right. Kalu Mia said to me, "Doug, Bhai, have
mercy on Kangal. Give him another chance. He will pay
you all he owes."

I was astonished. Here was a Muslim preaching the gospel to me. He reminded me of how much more often than
Kangal I had duped the Lord and received mercy. Mercy is
not shown in an act or two. Rather, it is an attitude of heart

that does not look at the balance due but at the bond needed to unite.

Rev. Douglas Venne, M.M.
(from Milwaukee, Wisconsin)
Philippines and Bangladesh

Some time ago, Eufrasio, an elder of an Aymara clan in the Altiplano of Peru, came to his parish priest and asked if he might use his house for a meeting. The priest assured him that it would be fine. Eufrasio thanked him and said, "We want you to be there as well."

When the day arrived, quite a number of Aymara folks came for the meeting. It seems there had been an incident that had angered people and resulted in many hurt feelings in the group. The elder stood before the group and asked one man to stand and tell his side of the story, which he did. He then asked someone of the opposite opinion to tell his version. After each had spoken, Eufrasio suggested a solution to the problem—and all agreed. He then asked each person present to give a sign of peace to everyone else in the room. When this was done he said, "Now this will never be mentioned again." All left quietly in peace.

Eufrasio then turned to the priest, thanked him for allowing them to use his house, and he too left.

"Now I have truly witnessed the sacrament of reconciliation," said the priest.

Sr. Helen Phillips, M.M.
(from Hollis, New York)
Bolivia, Peru, and the United States

Leo and Andrea Goicochea left their home in Baltimore in 1985 and went with their two children—Christie, seven years old, and Marco, four—to work as lay missionaries in Venezuela. They returned after six years of mission labor in one of the poorest slums of Caracas. Andy told the following story.

I worked with catechist formation. A French sister and I worked hard to put together a first-rate curriculum. Yet it was my catechists who taught me to forgive. After unjustly accusing one of the catechists, I felt horrible when I realized that I was in the wrong. I figured she would never be able to forgive me and treat me as a friend again. I was truly touched by her ability to forgive me so easily and not make me feel as if I had to make up for it.

Sometimes forgiveness seemed easier for the people we worked with. They were not so wrapped up in themselves or overconfident that they took such offense. They truly realized that we are all human and can make mistakes. This understanding makes forgiveness much easier. (AG)

Interfaith Dialogue

From his experience working with the Muslim community in Bangladesh, Fr. J. Lawrence Schanberger, M.M., from Baltimore, shares the following story.

It was our turn to have the annual eucharistic procession in our village of Tuital, Bangladesh. Everyone prepared diligently. The day before the procession a neighboring Christian village advised us that, because of some Christian-Muslim tensions there, we should not have the procession. Our villagers were very disturbed because they had prepared so well. I decided to ask my poor Muslim boatman, Sultan, to consult with his *malobi* (head of the mosque) about whether we should have the procession.

He quickly returned and said, "The *malobi* said, 'Not only *should* you have your procession, but you *must* have your procession.'" So, the procession was held, and it was more beautiful than ever. (JLS)

It's All in Your Mind

Glory be to him whose power, working in us, can do infi-
nitely more than we can ask or imagine. (Ephesians 3:20)

This quotation from Paul's letter to the Ephesians has
always been one of my favorite passages and one that I
believe has had a great influence on my life. One time a
crew member on a cruise ship made this real for me in a
way I could never have imagined. It was my second cruise
as a ship's chaplain. On my first trip I had had problems
saying mass for the crew. This mass is always late at night,
and this is when the ship moves faster, creating more movement. During my first trip the greater speed made me so
seasick that I had to call off the mass.

This second time, as I went below for mass with the crew,
I was not feeling good at all. In greeting them, I tried to be
casual, "My sea legs are not doing too well." Hearing that,
one member of the crew told me, "It's all in your mind." I
responded that I often say the same thing about golf, "It's
all in the mind, and that is what worries me." However, he
was not impressed with my attempt at humor. Sounding
somewhat annoyed, he repeated: "It's all in your mind. If
you think about it, you'll be sick; if you don't think about it,
you won't be." He said this with such authority that it made
an immediate and deep impression on me.

I immediately said to myself, "Well, I am about to celebrate the liturgy; if there is anything I should put my mind
to, it is this celebration." And so it was. The ship continued
to dip and rise, and while I was aware of that movement
from time to time, it only served as a reminder to me to pay
attention to what I was doing. As often as I had heard the
saying "It's all in the mind," it never had any real impact on

me until that evening. It worked and it continues to work, giving lie to one old adage, "You can't teach an old dog new tricks." (JAH)

Learning

The lowly will find ever more joy in Yahweh and the poorest of people will delight in the Holy One of Israel. (Isaiah 29:19)

One of the great benefits of being a missioner is what we learn about ourselves. Lay missioner Andy Goicochea, from Baltimore, shares what she learned from the poor in Venezuela.

People in Venezuela often greeted me with an expression that made me cringe, *perdone lo malo*. Basically this translates into "forgive my poverty" or the little I have. For years this was an attitude I tried to fix, thinking these people didn't value themselves and that they lacked self-confidence. But as I continued to receive their forgiveness for my many cultural errors, I came to understand that this wasn't self-deprecating behavior but rather true humility.

As North Americans, we have much to learn from the people we serve. We are trained or programmed to think we are the center of the universe and we are "in control"; if we "mess up," it is the end of the world. (AG)

Fr. John J. Ruessmann, M.M., from Camden, New Jersey, has worked with some of the poorest people in the Philippines and Venezuela. Most recently he has served with the Q'eqchis, a Mayan people of Guatemala. The following story recounts what he learned about social justice from the Q'eqchis when they were reflecting on the story of the unjust judge in Luke 18.

Guatemala has its share of corrupt officials, as do many countries around the world. In order to highlight the relevance of Jesus' ancient story in Luke 18, and to probe one

A relationship of love—Chile

possible approach in the struggle for God's kingdom among us, I suggested to some Q'eqchi lay leaders assembled for a meeting that we seek to pressure—respectfully and without violence—our mayor to great accountability. The goal would be that each year the mayor would publicly account for how much income the municipality had received and how that money had been spent.

No one objected to my proposal, and several people agreed that it certainly would be good if the mayor were accountable in some way. At the end of the session the discussion was left open ended, and we waited to see what would happen.

During the months that followed I made this same proposal to lay leaders in other parts of the parish. Each time there was a similar response. It was respectfully accepted and then seemingly buried. Finally, at one of these meetings a participant, Qawa' Beet, had sufficient confidence and courage to express to me what many others had undoubtedly been thinking and feeling.

He said, "Father John, do you remember what happened a few years ago with the mayor in Poptún [a nearby town]? Do you remember how three men, talking with the mayor in his office, had gotten into an argument with him? Then all of them walked outside and there, in front of the municipal building, the mayor took out a gun, shot and killed all three men."

Later, in reflecting on Qawa' Beet's words, I realized that I needed to lay aside my presumptions that were rooted in the experiences of a white, middle-class man from the United States. In the United States, protests against actions of elected municipal leaders might be futile, but for the most part, they are not dangerous.

On the other hand, living among the Q'eqchis I needed to appreciate and take into account how much that violent incident, which had occurred at least five years earlier, continued to influence the people I was serving. And that incident was only the tip of the iceberg for them, given the many kinds of abuse and violence that had been imposed on them over the centuries. I was reminded once again that I did not have all the answers to important questions. More and more I came to recognize the importance of continuing to seek patiently and creatively appropriate questions and responses. I needed to draw respectfully on the experiences, knowledge, sense of community, and wisdom of the Q'eqchi. (JJR)

Liturgy

*They regularly went to the Temple but met in their homes
for the breaking of the bread; they shared their food gladly
and generously. (Acts 2:46)*

Señor Pausolino Marquez, a veritable patriarch of the
barrio in Caracas, faithfully organized the Venezuelan custom of "Standing Up the Baby Jesus" every February 2. It
celebrates the end of the Christmas season and moving
on.

In my first year as pastor, Señor Marquez invited me to
take part in the celebration. What took place that night made
a great impression on me. The ceremony took about four
hours. The entire rosary was sung, but with interruptions
after each set of mysteries so that an abundance of food
and drink could be passed around. After the rosary the fid-
dlers played and people danced. All the time little children
scurried about. Friends gathered in groups to talk politics
or discuss other topics of concern. Then a procession began, led by the statue of the baby Jesus, who would be set
upright to show that he was growing up. Then there was
more music and dancing and also a collection, marking this
clearly as a Catholic service.

During the entire evening I never saw Señor Marquez
actually do anything other than nod to one of his children
and then to another, and then something else would begin
to happen. It dawned on me that I was witnessing an example of the kind of early Christian liturgy we read about
in Paul's writings or Acts. While Señor Marquez was the
president of the assembly, he did not have to do everything.
His job was simply to see that it was done, that it was a
community celebration. This is what liturgy should be, I
thought to myself.

It's important to point out that Venezuelan *barrios* can be very dangerous places. Because of this, Señor Marquez had built a kind of enclave in which his house was in the center and the houses of seven of his children were built around it. Despite the danger, he insisted that everyone in the *barrio* was welcome that night, and this included the local thugs. Of course, his sons and sons-in-law kept watchful eyes, but the night and the celebration went by without incident. It was a house celebration in a Caracas slum that continued until midnight, and everyone was welcome. (JAH)

The following story by Fr. Vincent P. Cole, from Detroit, Michigan, appeared in *Once Upon a Time in Asia*, edited by James H. Kroeger, M.M., and Eugene F. Thalman, M.M. Fr. Cole works in Papua, Indonesia.

The Muyu tribe of Irian-Jaya are a people who are tenacious, thrifty, superstitious, and often strongly opinionated. A Catholic priest, a friend of mine, reflected on the dilemma of preaching to them. "Isn't it strange," he said, "that we come halfway across the world to preach about God to the Muyu tribe? We herd people of every sex and age into the church and proceed to reveal to them God's sacred mysteries. We shout words over the din of a noisy congregation, often using loudspeakers, in order to get across this most sacred of messages. The louder we make it, the better it seems.

"What must the Muyu people think? It is a frontal attack on their way of dealing with the sacred. For the Muyu, the most sacred of mysteries must be transmitted via revered whispers directly from mouth to ear. The mysteries must be revealed in stages, starting with the elders and ending with the young people, but only when they are judged able to absorb the profundity of the material. It is only the most innocuous of messages that can be discussed openly before young and old, male and female alike. To do this with the sacred is disrespectful. It prompts one to doubt the veracity of the content." (VPC)

Love

No one can have greater love than to lay down his life for his friends. (John 15:13)

The best gentleman I ever met did not fit the image of a gentleman. In the unlikely event that he would have ever walked into the average parish church, people might very well have jumped out through the stained-glass windows. A homeless man in Tokyo, he looked like what he was, one of life's casualties. He had one eye, and not many more teeth. He had not been near a bath in years, and his clothes were torn, greasy, and stinking. His hair stuck out from his head in filthy spikes. He kept himself in food and drink by collecting scrap cardboard in a cart and selling it to recyclers.

Yet, he was a gentleman. Every day he went to a soup kitchen in the district in which he lived. Most of those who came ate and left, and many would offer thanks for their meal. This man always made it a point to visit the volunteers in the kitchen, asking them how far they had traveled to help out and thanking them in the most cultured and polite language for their generosity.

One winter day he came with an injured man in his cart. The injured man had been struck by a car, and his foot was hurt. The center had a free clinic, and the doctor on duty examined him. There was a broken bone in his foot, but the injured man refused to go to a hospital for treatment. (The homeless frequently fear hospitals because they seldom get to one before it is too late for them to be helped. As a result they think hospitals are places where they will die.) The doctor agreed that complete rest outside a hospital bed would eventually work as well as rest in such a bed, so he did not try to force the man into a hospital.

From that day on, the gentleman cared for the injured man. The cart became a mobile home for him. For six weeks the gentleman gave his food to the patient. Since his cart was being used as a hospital bed on wheels, the gentleman could not work to earn even his usual poor living.

Then, one cold morning, the injured man woke up and shook the gentleman to wake him. He was dead. Six weeks of giving up most of his food and six weeks of sleeping on the winter sidewalk in order that his friend might sleep in the cart had cost him his life.

In the Gospel of John, Jesus says, "No one can have greater love than to lay down his life for his friends." When I learned of the gentleman's death, I was embarrassed. After all, I know these words of Jesus. I know the promise of eternal life. I am a Christian. Yet here was a man who may never have heard of Christ, but who did what I have never had the faith and courage to do. A common caricature of Catholics includes big doses of guilt. I certainly fit the caricature then, and to some extent I still do when I think of that gentleman.

Over the years, as I thought more, I realized that the gentleman and I had something in common. He was without doubt a saint, but that's not what we have in common. "Without doubt" does not fit my case; confident of God's grace, I only hope to be received at the end. What we have in common is imperfection. His problems and imperfections were obvious to anyone who looked. Mine might be better disguised, yet even so, they are prominent—to me at least.

Isn't it true that we tend to see what is lacking in our lives, in our faith? The missing, broken part of my life overshadows the child of God that I am. The gentleman's case was the same. Anyone who looked at him saw only the dirt and homelessness, missing entirely the saint who lived in their shadow. From childhood on, people point out our shortcomings. Ask any child (or adult, for that matter) to make a list of his or her failings, and one sheet of paper will not be enough. Ask the same people to list their qualities that show them to be sons and daughters of God, and when the list finally appears after much hemming, hawing, and crossing out, it will be short. We often view others the same way, seeing only their weaknesses and imperfections and missing the image of God that is the basic reality of every human life.

In the Acts of the Apostles, Peter sees that God's love will not be limited: "I begin to see how true it is that God shows no partiality" (Acts 10:34). God showed love through that gentleman in Tokyo. God can, and does, show that same love through me as well.

"Love, then, consists in this: not that we have loved God, but that God has loved us and has sent the Son as an offering for our sins," says John in his epistle. All humankind is embraced by that love.

We must make an effort to see the children of God hidden in our families, our friends, our foes, strangers, and even ourselves. Let's look beyond the problems, sins, and weakness in ourselves and others to see how great God's love is. As Christians who have been chosen to know and proclaim the Son, we are especially blessed. Among our blessings is the knowledge of who it is that acts in women and men such as the Tokyo gentleman. So, let's give thanks for God's love that overflows the church and shows itself through saints beyond our community—saints we might not even recognize at first glance.

Fr. William J. Grimm, M.M.
(from New York City)
Japan and the United States

Ministry Reversed

*With him went the Twelve, as well as certain women who
had been cured of evil spirits and ailments: Mary sur-
named the Magdalene, from whom seven demons had gone
out, Johanna the wife of Herod's steward Chuza, Susanna,
and many others who provided for them out of their own
resources. (Luke 8:2–3)*

Sister Bernadette Lynch, M.M., from Brooklyn, worked for.many
years in Peru. Here she shares an experience of reverse ministry.

Reach out! Touch someone with your compassion and
love! How often had it been drilled into us as we entered
each new phase of our mission journey. And I often
reached out to parishioners upon hearing that someone
in their family had had an accident or illness or died. I
never hesitated to reach out and embrace them, and hope-
fully they felt the warmth of my love and concern.

But I will never forget that early morning when I was
on my way down to mass in Juli, Peru. As usual, one of
my neighbors was standing at the door of her adobe house.
Each morning she would ask me about my father, who
was very ill. She did not know that the previous evening
one of the Maryknoll brothers had driven from Puno to
tell me that word had just arrived that my father had died
that morning in New York. When she asked me about him
that morning, I told her my sad news, and her arms immediately went around me as I cried and cried on her
shoulder. I had been living alone at that time, and it had
been a long time since I had felt the warmth and love from
someone else after offering that love and compassion so

often myself. I received it with deep and everlasting gratitude. (BL)

Fr. Robert A. Jalbert, M.M., from Worcester, Massachusetts, was ordained in 1979. He is presently assigned to the Promotion Department at Society headquarters having recently returned from his mission in Africa. The following account is from his experience in the slums of Nairobi, Kenya.

The hundreds of thousands of people like Maria who live in these "informal settlements" in Nairobi are for the most part doing so illegally, literally "squatting" on government land. At any time and with little or no warning, the government can demolish their simple dwellings and throw them off of the land. When that happens, most of these people have nowhere else to go. The government of Kenya was talking about doing just this in Kibera in March 2003 while I was ministering there with the Guadalupe Missionaries. One morning I was visiting with Maria, and we had this very brief conversation:

Fr. Bob: "Maria, what is it like to live here each day with no housing security, not knowing whether or not the government is going to come in and demolish your home and throw you out, but knowing that if this happens you have nowhere else to go?"

Maria: "You know, Father, my family and I are very grateful to God because we're not poor and sick at the same time. We're just poor."

I literally had no response for Maria's simple but profound statement. What could I have said? Maria reminded me that in her daily life the glass is half full rather than half empty. And this is the attitude and deeply felt belief of most of these people who face such difficulties. She helped me to see that she and her children do not complain to God or to others about their material poverty or their lack of housing security, but rather that they recognize that the good health they enjoy comes from a loving and caring God and that it is important to give thanks to God for the gifts that one has in life. At that moment I, who had gone to proclaim the good news to Maria, had the good news proclaimed to me. (RAJ)

Nativity Scene:
An African Correction

The rich may think himself wise, but the intelligent poor will unmask him. (Proverbs 28:11)

Fr. John E. Conway, M.M., from New York City, was a Christian Brother before joining Maryknoll and being ordained. He served in Nairobi and the United States. He taught school for many years, but a little African girl in turn taught him a valuable lesson from her culture.

On December 28 I stood before a nativity scene in my parish's church in Musoma, Tanzania, with a girl of five years. Maryanne said to me, "Padri John, there is something wrong with this picture." I looked again but saw only the familiar nativity scene with the holy family. Maryanne insisted, so I looked again. Finally I asked, "Maryanne, what is wrong?" She replied, "No one is holding the child!"

In Tanzania children are always held or even strapped on the back of their mothers and siblings. They are never simply looked at. (JEC)

A mother holds her baby in a chapel—Shinyanga, Tanzania

Patience

Naked I came from my mother's womb, naked I shall return again. Yahweh gave, Yahweh has taken back. Blessed be the name of Yahweh. (Job 1:21)

Fr. Donald F. Sybertz, M.M., of Boston has dedicated his entire mission life to the service of the church in Africa. He has also dedicated many years to collecting stories of faith of the African people. The following article is taken from *Towards an African Narrative Theology,* a book that Fr. Sybertz wrote in collaboration with his fellow missioner, Fr. Joseph G. Healey.

There was a doctor at Bugando Hospital in Mwanza, Tanzania, named Mwana Mayombi, which means "the son of Mayombi." He encountered terrible problems in his personal life. First, his aunt, who was suffering from cancer, was brought to him at the hospital. While he was taking care of her, Dr. Mayombi received news that rustlers had stolen his cattle in his home village. So he left his aunt in the care of the other doctors and went home to find out about the theft.

When he arrived home, he received a telephone call from the hospital saying that his aunt had died. "Bring her home," he said. The other doctors brought her body home. While he was busy preparing for his aunt's burial, Dr. Mayombi got a telephone call telling him that a fire had gutted his house. His only question was, "Is everyone safe?" They answered, "Yes."

Shortly after his aunt's funeral, he received a telephone call from Dar es Salaam saying that his daughter had died in a car accident. Dr. Mayombi told them to bring her body home for burial, too.

After burying his daughter, Dr. Mayombi asked his father for a Bible. He opened to the Book of Job and read. When he finished reading, Dr. Mayombi said to his father and his relatives, "When I came out of my mother's stomach all I had was given to me by God. Now God has taken back what belongs to God. My aunt died, my cattle were stolen, my house was gutted by fire, my daughter died. But I continue to thank God for all He has given me. I am not going to bother myself about the loss of my cattle. I will go back to work at the hospital."

But his father and relatives tried to prevent him from going back to work before settling the case of the cattle. They said, "You should go to a diviner to find out the cause of your problems." Dr. Mayombi's response was, "No, I accept everything as part of God's plan. God is in charge of my life, not the witches."

Three times he said to his family, "Please let me go." Finally, they agreed to let him go back to work at Bugando Hospital. Dr. Mayombi was able to bear the pain of his losses with the grace of God. They called him "Little Job." (DFS)

Poverty

Fr. Thomas H. Keefe, M.M., of Newark, New Jersey, went to East Africa after ordination in 1955 and worked there for thirteen years before returning to the United States to work in the Education Department of Maryknoll. In the following article he is not quoting anyone in particular but rather reflecting on what he heard the African people saying with their lives.

It is true that we African people are in many ways poor, very poor, and that our family living is simple and has many weaknesses and deficiencies when compared with living styles of people in other parts of our world, styles that we see in the pictures of magazines from Europe and America.

But, please, don't overlook our strengths, our special wisdom, our dignity, and our pride in the way we live life. We do have many weaknesses in our living and in our culture, but we also have our strengths, and such strengths are mostly within our family and tribal living and can be described in this way:

> In times of lacking the necessities of life,
> In times of sickness with no medicine,
> In times of hunger with little food,
> In times of longing without opportunity,
> We have remarkable patience—and
> such patience can be a good example to all
> the world.

And we can give the world our example of real joy. We greet one another, not just because we have to but because we are happy to meet. There is little prejudice in our attitudes. There is genuine laughter in our gatherings and deep joy in our being together. We have real joy most of the

A family at mass in a Nairobi slum—Kenya

time and we have a special "African joy" with the rest of the world.

We have a simple and uncomplicated way of life. This way of living could bring more happiness to many in our world. People of more "advanced" cultures compete for wealth and power. We people of Africa are strong. It is wrong to say that we are weak just because we are poor. We are strong. We work the entire day in the hot sun to plant and harvest our daily food. Our lives are filled with struggle and hardship and sickness, and yet we face these challenges bravely because we are strong.

And we have deep faith. We receive few material rewards for our believing yet we almost instinctively trust in a good God who is important to us in so many ways. Even those of us outside of any organized religions have a sense of the God of heaven and earth as being important to us and good to us in so many ways.

When we pray, we pray with all our hearts. When we sing, we sing with all our strength. It is said at times that we almost lift off the roof of the church with the volume and the power of our song. And we carry our faith from our mission churches to every part of our life and our living. We do this because we have faith. (THK)

Prayer

If you have faith, everything you ask for in prayer, you will receive. (Matthew 21:22)

Her name was Rosa, and the weekly Bible group was to meet in her house the following week on the theme of prayer. Rosa came to the rectory, looking for one of the priests in our parish who might be willing to offer some instruction on the subject. So I put some ideas together, typed them out, and went to the Monday evening session where eight members of the community had gathered.

I began by asking about their experiences of prayer. (Perhaps it was the Holy Spirit who prompted me to use this Socratic approach rather than one that was didactic.) It was Rosa who went first.

"Well," she began, "the first thing I do in the morning is to thank God for another day and for keeping us safe during the night because there is so much violence in our neighborhood. Then I try to sing little hymns as I make breakfast. When my husband goes out to work, I pray for his safety because he's a policeman in Caracas. Then as I send the children off to school, I pray for their safety too, and that they will behave. I talk to God all day long about all the things that we need, like clothing for the children, and I tell God about the things that worry me. I tell God how lonely I get because I haven't seen my mother in three years because she lives in the Sucre State. Sometimes I get angry that God doesn't answer, like when I asked for help with my niece who is running with really bad company. She got pregnant, and we don't know where she is. Once I didn't speak to God for a whole afternoon because I was so mad, and I told God just how mad I was. Then I felt bad about that and said that I was sorry. I really don't know what prayer is. I just talk to God."

I don't know whether it was her authenticity or her vulnerability, but that short description about her own life of prayer led the others in the group to open up and share their experiences. I was very grateful to them all as I quietly slipped my prepared notes under the chair. (JAH)

A Protestant in a Catholic Mission?

One of the first weddings that I officiated at in St. Andrew's parish, Newtown, Pennsylvania, was that of Frank Manzo and Linda Pfeiffer in December 1961. We became very good friends, and nine years later when I was working in Valencia, Venezuela, they came down with their four children and worked a year with us. Frank, who was fluent in Spanish, was a teacher in the local high school and had also been a catechist at St. Andrew's. Linda was Methodist and had only had a basic course in Spanish in college.

Although grateful for the tremendous commitment they were making, I was concerned about how Linda would fit in. How would this young woman, coming from a comfortable suburban background, handle living in a government apartment that we had furnished with secondhand tables, chairs, beds, and so on?

Linda not only survived the year but made a powerful impression on the people. How did she do it? She decided to make it a learning experience, asking her neighbors how to prepare *arepas* (cornmeal biscuits with meat or cheese that are a staple in the Venezuelan diet), how to wax the raw cement floors of the apartment, or what to do when a child came down with a fever. Of course the neighbor women were delighted to show how they do things, and so they established a mutually respectful relationship very quickly. That is how it first dawned on me that it is essential for the missioner to learn from the very people he or she is going to teach. It levels the ground and shows your respect for the other culture and for your hosts. (JAH)

Role Model

Slum parishes in Venezuela are not easy places to work. When you have a North American agenda, nothing seems to fit together the way you think it should. I have to admit to more than a little frustration while working in Santa Cruz Parish in Caracas in the mid-1970s. A good example is shown in my experience one day when a parishioner approached me to ask for a favor. It was José Domingo Muñoz, one of the greatest collaborators that any parish ever had, a man who was always there when you needed something. He asked if I would drive him on Sunday to visit his parents, whom he had not seen in a long time. He added that Sunday was the only day he did not have to work. José Domingo was not the kind of person who took advantage of people, and I felt that I owed him a lot, so we set off on a one-hour trek to a neighboring town.

On the way he told me that his mother was eighty-six years old and his father was ninety-nine. As we drove up to the house, his father was working in the garden. Hearing more than seeing our car, the elderly man started toward us, still unsure about who his visitors were because he was nearly blind. The thick lenses of his heavy-rimmed glasses resembled the bottoms of a soda bottle. Once he recognized his son, his eyes lit up and he gave him a big *abrazo* (embrace). After giving me an equally strong *abrazo*, he led us into the house.

It was a government-constructed rural structure, very simple in every way. As he shuffled more than walked, he showed us his collections of saints and then led us into the kitchen where his wife was preparing lunch. He put his arm around her and said, "Father, meet my little girl." "*Mi muchachita*" he called her as he gave her a little hug. It struck me that here is a ninety-nine-year-old man who is still in love!

An elderly man—Central America

I thought long and hard that day as we returned to Caracas. Bartolo Muñoz was the opposite of all that this world considers important, and yet he was about the happiest man I had ever met. He was poor, short, bald, nearly blind, partially deaf, and with very black skin in a culture that still suffers from residual racism. Whether he knew of all those prejudices I do not know. But, even if he did, they certainly did not affect him. He was genuinely a very happy man, and I knew that I owed him a great debt for how he helped me reorganize some personal priorities.

Bartolo Muñoz did not live to celebrate his one hundred years but slipped away quietly just one month before his birthday. For the viewing his family had attached a small cross to each prayer card, and I still have the little cross as a reminder of what brings happiness and what does not.

Epilogue: Two years after her husband's death, Mrs. Muñoz was felled with a stroke. When I got the call on the parish phone, I went for José Domingo and we drove to the family home with no knowledge of the severity of her condition. As we entered the dwelling, his mother was lying very still on a small cot. I stepped back as José Domingo approached the cot and knelt down next to his mother. When she didn't move, José Domingo asked, "Mama, do you know who I am?" She answered, "No." He responded, "I am José Domingo, your son." To which she opened one eye, winked at him, and said, "Well, if you know who you are, why did you ask me?" (JAH)

Sharing

Keep doing good works and sharing your resources, for these are the kinds of sacrifices that please God. (Hebrews 13:16)

I am a secondary-school teacher, so when I was asked to "take care of" a second-grade class while the teacher was at a meeting, I cringed. What could I do with fifty little people? Arriving in the classroom I saw that the teacher had left work for the children to do. It was absolutely quiet. Each one was writing away except for one little boy. I went over to him and said, "Why aren't you writing like the other children?" He quickly replied, "I don't have a pencil." The boy sitting next to him said nothing but quickly broke his own pencil in two and handed half of it to his friend and then went right back to his own work.

I was amazed! He didn't hesitate one moment about giving half of what he possessed to his friend. He had a bigger pencil than he needed, and his friend had none. It was so spontaneous! Watching them side by side, I wondered if my sense of generosity, of sharing, came even near to his. What a lesson I learned! By the way, the receiver of the pencil whipped out a little razor blade (a poor boy's version of a pencil sharpener), sharpened the dull end, and began his work.

Sr. Helen Phillips, M.M.
(from Hollis, New York)
Bolivia, Peru, and the United States

We were never sure of the woman's correct name because she seemed to give a different answer each time she was asked, but we will call her Julia. Although she lived only fifty yards away, the first time she appeared in the chapel was the night we had a general meeting to discuss the problems in the *barrio*. Her only son was one of the local thugs in Barinas (Venezuela), and she had gone to the meeting because she apparently suspected there would be talk about setting up a vigilante system.

Happy to learn that that was not the issue, she left, but not before hearing about our breakfast program. She wondered if she could take part. Of course we welcomed her and she began to come every morning. After some weeks had gone by, the director of the program told me that Julia had been eating only half of her *arepa* and walking out with the other half. When questioned about it, she said that she was taking the other half to an elderly neighbor who had nothing to eat and could not walk to our hall. Although we had a rule that all food had to be consumed on the premises, we made an exception and always allowed Julia to take a whole *arepa* to her neighbor. (JAH)

Water is very scarce in the slums of Caracas. Sometimes it would come every two or three weeks, and then everyone filled up every can and oil drum that could be found to preserve it. One day as I was visiting a family one of the children came in and said that their neighbor had asked to "borrow" a pail of water. I wondered what the mother would answer, because she had seven children and her husband worked on construction. I thought of what it must mean to clean, wash clothes and dishes, and take baths with whatever water they had. Yet she never hesitated but only asked her son, "Do we have any?"

When he said, "Yes, we have a tub full," she immediately replied, "Then give her some."

What struck me was the lack of any hesitation on her part. All she asked was if, indeed, they had any water to give. I thought of some of the responses that would have been possible about having to cook and wash for so many people. But the woman never hesitated at all. (JAH)

One day, while visiting the families in my village of Tuital, Bangladesh, a poor little girl came running out of her house with a beautiful little flower in her hand. She said, "This is for you, Father," and then ran back into her house, smiling and happy. I realized that this flower was all that she had to give me. With great care I carried the delicate little flower back to my house. But what I noticed before arriving home was that this flower, a gift of this poor Christian child, had brought smiles and greetings from everyone along the road: Hindus, Muslims, and Christians. It had been a moment of peace and joy for everyone!

Fr. J. Lawrence Schanberger, M.M.
(from Baltimore)
Chile, Venezuela, the United States,
and Bangladesh

Fr. Thomas J. Dunleavy, M.M., was born in Ireland but resided in Baltimore before joining Maryknoll. His mission career has taken him to the Philippines, North Vietnam, Thailand, and Cambodia. He has worked extensively with refugees.

One morning when the holding center for new refugees was very crowded, I noticed a young Thai man talking with the Africans. One of the African men said that he was going home that afternoon but that he had no shoes. The young Thai man reached down, removed his own shoes, and gave them to the African. Then, he said goodbye and walked away in his bare feet. (TJD)

Dave and Sharon Raynor left the United States with their three sons in 1982. Dave Jr. was seven, Mike was five, and Brian, one year old. In 1985 their daughter, Katie, was born in the local hospital in Barquisimeto, Venezuela. Their two major projects were a food cooperative, La Feria, and a health center. Both programs continue today although the Raynors left their mission in 1993 to return to the United States for work in home missions.

Sharon explained their experience: "I would definitely say that our years in Venezuela had a profound affect on all of us and gave direction to the rest of our lives. Our experience there gave us a worldview that is so much wider and that takes into account the life experience of the majority of people in the world, those who live in poverty. Our children in particular have benefited from the experience of being raised in another culture and have all been involved in international justice issues and volunteer work giving service to the most needy. We are indeed extremely grateful to Maryknoll and to the Venezuelan people for giving us the opportunity to stretch and expand our minds and hearts."

One of the most important lessons I learned during my seven years in Venezuela is that our personal happiness is not tied to the amount of money or belongings we have. In my childhood I was taught—as were most Americans—that the more I had, the happier I would be. And in fact I was very happy with my upper-middle-class life in the United States. I assumed that a good part of my happiness could be attributed to the fact that I had "made it" in the eyes of the world.

When I first arrived in Venezuela, I could not speak the language very well, and I spent a lot of time reading the faces of people I encountered for clues about what they were saying. Inevitably, I saw happy faces almost everywhere I went. Even those folks who were living in shacks without running water or electricity looked happier than many people with unlimited purchasing power I knew in Westchester County, a wealthy suburban area of New York.

The Venezuelans were dependent on friends and neighbors for survival, a reality that would be shameful in our U.S. culture, which prizes individualism and independence above all else. Yet that very dependence strengthened the relationship with their friends and neighbors and helped form community bonds that went very deep. These folks, who had very little to celebrate from the point of view of U.S. society, could party like no one I had known before. Their happiness came from within, from their strong faith, which made them secure in God's love for them, and not from the size of their house or their paycheck. I learned that our human capacity to be generous and share what we have been gifted with in life diminishes in proportion to the material wealth we possess. The poorer we are, it seems, the greater our ability to welcome the stranger for a meal and share the little we have.

On the second day after moving into the *barrio* several children were playing at our house, and I gave little Lucelia, who was five years old and one of sixteen children in her family, two cookies to eat. I still remember being totally flabbergasted when she turned around and immediately shared one of them with my son Michael, who didn't have any. This was a little girl who had probably only had a few cookies in her lifetime, but she handed one to Michael without a second thought simply because he didn't have one and she had two. She totally shattered my preconception of poor people as those who would understandably want to hoard what little they had for themselves.

The lesson in generosity that I was taught by little Lucelia was repeated on an almost daily basis as we visited with our neighbors in the *barrio* in the following months. There were times when I was astonished by the generous giving spirit of the poor. When a tornado passed through and destroyed several hundred tin and cardboard shacks in the neighboring *barrio,* our neighbors brought bags of food and clothing to our house, which served as a distribution center. I was amazed once again at the incredible generosity of folks who had very little themselves but were willing to give from their own poverty to folks they had never met but who had an even greater need. They truly lived out the gospel story of the widow's mite in their ability to give from their essence and not their excess. I was truly gifted by the generous and giving ways of the Venezuelan people, and I pray that I can be more like them in sharing my material riches. (SR)

After having spent some time serving a local Christian community in the Philippines, I was leaving for a new assignment. One of the local community leaders, a single mother with several children, was feeling bad about my leaving. It was evident that she was very poor.

As I was leaving she came up to me and gave me a gift of dark, overripe bananas. My first impulse was to return the bananas to her, for I presumed that she could hardly afford them and she had children to feed. However, I decided to accept them, for I realized that any refusal on my part would hurt her. She was providing a very generous gift, and she wanted (and perhaps needed) to express her gratitude to me for my service to the community. Needless to say I was deeply touched by her caring "going away" gift.

Fr. Thomas Marti, M.M.
(from Seattle, Washington)
Philippines and the United States

Even though a missioner respects and admires the customs of the host country and tries to learn from them, it may not always be possible to incorporate them into his or her own culture. The following experience of Fr. Michael O. Zunno, M.M., from his nearly fifty years as a missioner in Korea, serves as an example of a custom that one may admire in another culture but not one that a person would necessarily imitate. Fr. Zunno is originally from Brooklyn, New York.

While dining with guests in their home, Fr. Mike noticed that when some unexpected friends of the family arrived, another guest, not the host, invited the newly arrived to be seated and to help themselves. Although the man was not the host but rather a guest in someone else's house, he felt free to invite others to sit down and take part in the meal. This was quite a surprise to the American missioner. He said that there is a saying in Korea: "The lessons learned at three years of age last until eighty." However, he could never bring himself to invite someone to sit down in a house that was not his.

Then, it happened to Fr. Mike himself. He told us the story of a Thanksgiving when he had guests, including a Korean seminarian. "In comes a friend of the seminarian, and he was immediately invited to sit down. I didn't care what food he was offered except for a small portion of creamed onions that I wanted to horde for myself. Lo and behold, the seminarian gave them to the newly arrived guest. I should have learned more about generosity from the Koreans!" (MOZ)

I was always impressed by the Africans I worked with in Tanzania and Kenya. Their capacity to share and their generosity seem to strike everyone who visits. One day I had a chance to see how early they learn to be so spontaneously generous when I met a lovely young mother who was talking to a small child securely wrapped on her back. Her other children were working alongside her, and we were all having a nice conversation. I offered the little one a small sweet candy, and the child held it out to the mother for a lick and then offered the candy to each of the siblings for a lick before enjoying it. I was amazed and realized that sharing had become a fixed part of their lives from the time they were very young.

Fr. Thomas P. McDonnell, M.M.
(from Brooklyn, New York)
Kenya, Tanzania, and the United States

One Tuesday afternoon I participated in the Bible reflections of a small Christian community at the home of

Member of a small Christian community—Tanzania

Theresa, one of the most faithful Christians in Bukiriro Village in Tanzania. Following local African custom, she had prepared a place outdoors for us to pray together. She arranged straw mats in a circle and placed fresh flowers in a vase in the middle. Obviously embarrassed, Theresa hesitated to place her only crucifix next to the flowers. It was old and made of plastic and had no arms. It had probably been brought to Tanzania by a missioner many years before and been passed around by several families. I said to Theresa, "Don't worry. The crucifix is fine. I am sure it has a special meaning for us."

One of the leaders read the Lenten gospel. This was followed by a period of silence and shared reflections. Suddenly it dawned on us what that old, battered, armless crucifix was saying. Jesus was asking us to be his arms and to reach out to the poor, the needy, the sick, the suffering, the oppressed. Several Christians shared their thoughts on this, emphasizing the importance of mutual help in our local community. One person quoted a favorite Swahili saying, "Words without actions are useless."

After the Bible service, we helped Anna, one of our neighbors who had two sick children. We gathered firewood and fetched water for her while she stayed at home with her children. Like Jesus, we tried to be men and women for others.

Fr. Joseph G. Healey, M.M.
(from Baltimore)
Kenya and Tanzania

Suffering

In the Jesus Caritas Fraternity we say a prayer every day that was written by Blessed Charles de Foucauld. One line of the prayer has always caused me some personal concern because I doubt my ability to say it with sincerity. It reads, "Whatever You may do, I thank You." I wonder if this means that I should be thankful for cancer, for insults, for some thug putting a knife in my stomach to get my money? Should I really be thankful? Then I recall a hospital visit many years ago.

I visited a young father of three children who earned his living as a roofer. One day he slipped and fell backward into a vat of pitch. I visited him the next day in the hospital, and I have to say that I never saw anyone in such pain. Evidently morphine cannot totally eliminate such severe pain, but the young father did not complain. As he talked about his accident, he said something that I will never forget. His words were, "You know, Father, this is really painful and I wonder how it happened, but then I have to say that I am grateful to God that it happened to me and not to one of my children." I am not usually at a loss for words, but that day the power of his experience left me speechless. (JAH)

Surprises

Fr. John J. McAuley, M.M., from Brooklyn, New York, worked as a missioner in Japan. In 1992 he began work with the United Nations and was later appointed as director of Social Communications for Maryknoll. Elected to Maryknoll's General Council in 2002 , he is presently serving in China.

The greater part of my mission experience in Japan took place on Hokkaido, the northernmost island of the archipelago. Hokkaido is blessed with a number of excellent ports that serve primarily internal commercial traffic. However, there are also a few ports that are designated for foreign trade. Third-world countries are the chief users of these ports, but Japan's closest neighbors on her northern borders, China, the Koreas, and Russia, also make regular runs to these ports for off-loading and on-loading raw materials.

Shortly after my arrival in August 1983 to start my assignment in the busy port city of Tomakomai, I joined with a small group of interfaith leaders to begin an outreach to foreign seafarers. A large part of this ministry consisted of visiting the seafarers on board their ships, and I thoroughly enjoyed this opportunity to get to know so many people from around the world.

About a year into this work one of my colleagues observed that I never visited any Russian ships (then the Soviet Union). I responded that this was probably just a coincidence, and he countered that he did not think so, that even when the opportunity arose, I never took advantage of it. He asked if there was a reason I never boarded a Soviet ship. Surprised by this observation, I volunteered to visit the next Russian ship to come into port.

As I walked up the steep gangplank of the large Soviet vessel a week later, I began to feel uncomfortable, and doubts arose that had not occurred to me when making other ship visits: How would these men respond to me, knowing that I was a priest? Would they be belligerent, or worse? And so it came as a shock to me to be given one of the most unrestricted permissions for unaccompanied access to a ship by a captain. My surprise deepened when the seafarers came with small gifts of sweets and drink for me and showed me pictures of their families with smiles of great pride. Some even surreptitiously flashed some small holy cards for me to glimpse so I would know that they were believers. One man whispered in my ear that he had learned some prayers from his grandmother, and someone else asked if I could go to his quarters later for confession. A group asked if a Catholic priest could say mass for non–Roman Catholics if they got to town before leaving port.

And then I realized that I *had* been avoiding Soviet ships, that I was both deeply afraid and highly resentful of those who manned the ships. It became clear to me that twenty-one years before, beginning with the Cuban missile crisis in October 1962 when I was only ten years old, I had learned how the "godless, atheistic Russian" communists hated us and hated religion. Once again I remembered saying goodbye to my parents during the height of the crisis; at the time I didn't know if we would see each other again, all because of the Russians. I also remembered having that fear reinforced again and again each time we practiced escape procedures at school in case of bombing attacks.

I carried that unconscious fear and hate within me unabated for twenty-one years, until a group of welcoming seafarers showed me their humanity, a humanness that was as warm and vulnerable as mine or of any other person I have met. (JJM)

Teachers Become Learners

Fr. William T. O'Leary, M.M., of Trenton, New Jersey, has had one of the most extensive mission experiences at Maryknoll. His first assignment was to Korea, where he learned to speak Korean like a native. He was elected to the General Council of Maryknoll in 1972 and later took up missions in Thailand, Indonesia, and finally in East Timor, where he had to study Portuguese before tackling the native language. Fr. O'Leary passed away in February 2007.

To my great surprise I gained a huge insight from a group of Thai farmers back in 1983. I had just arrived in Thailand and was starting an agricultural project. Maryknoll had received an invitation to take on a new mission in the Mekong area of South East Asia. Although I had finished formal language school, I could barely get along in Thai. However, my biggest worry was not a linguistic one but a farming one. I knew nothing at all about farming. During my six months of language study I read every book on agriculture that was available, but it was of no use. Our farm project in the Mekong area included every conceivable dimension of agriculture: crops, orchards, animals, fowl, fish ponds, whatever.

I was dead in the water. But I did have one asset that I hadn't really anticipated, and it was the wisdom of the Thai farmers who would be my neighbors. I had seen them as the targets of the project rather than the doers or enablers.

I arrived at the chosen site for the project, built a fence around it, and started to grade the land as best I could. With that done, the hard part started. What seeds to buy? When to plant what? Which end of a seed went up and which went down? How deep to plant the silly things? And on and on.

A rice farmer—Cambodia

My Thai neighbors came to watch for a few days, and they soon realized that I knew nothing at all and they offered to help. They were afraid that I'd die of starvation right on my own farm. Each day they came to teach me. Little by little, crops got planted, chickens got put in coops, pigs were in sties, and fish ponds got dug and stocked. Even more than that, I became great friends with those neighbors, all of whom were Buddhist.

A little reflection on that experience revealed a lot. In nearly all of Asia, people are greatly influenced by Confucian rules of reverence within the community. The mutual relationships of father and child, king and subject, teacher and disciple, and so on are all extremely important. Unconsciously, I had placed myself as a disciple to those neighbors, my farmer teachers, and they were very much at home with that. They were the ones with knowledge and skills, and they became my teachers. I was no longer the usual foreign missioner who comes with a whole agenda to teach.

As I thought about it, I realized that if this sort of relationship-building works with farming projects in Asia, it might also work in other fields of interaction. Instead of designing and running a parish or project personally, we could involve the people in its design and administration. Rather than our deciding unilaterally on the humanitarian needs of the people and how they might be met, why not invite the people to describe their own needs? Instead of teaching religion out of our Western magisterial treasure house, why not open the treasures of Eastern spirituality, get familiar with them, and change catechetical ministry into a dialogue rather than a monologue? In other words, I was being challenged to get down off my professorial pedestal and learn the wonders of ministry. (WTO)

Fr. Francis T. McGourn, M.M., from Philadelphia, Pennsylvania, was sent for linguistic studies after his ordination in 1964. In 1974, with the assistance of a Peruvian, Victor Ochoa, the son of a healer/prayer person, he founded the Institute of Aymaran Studies in Puno, Peru. He later became the director of the Maryknoll Language Institute in Cochabamba, Bolivia, and in 2002 he was elected vicar general of Maryknoll. He has since returned to Cochabamba.

When I worked for nine years among the Aymaras of the Altiplano of Peru, they shared their faith with me in a very effective and, for me, surprising way. I went to Peru with the idea that the Aymaras knew little about God, Jesus, or the Christian faith. The first few years that I worked with them did little to change my impression. I constantly saw examples of a religious faith and of ritual practices that convinced me more and more each day that these "poor Indians" were very confused in their beliefs. I considered them to be tied down to their myths, their rites, their syncretistic beliefs that led them to confuse Mother Earth with the Mother of God, the saints with pagan gods, and so on. I was convinced that I would have to study a lot about them, their history, and their beliefs to be able to help them arrive at an adequate understanding of and a correct expression of the Christian faith. In other words, I wanted to find ways to make them think and act like me.

My studies yielded a lot of data and facts about the Aymaras. The data was verifiable, and I could not understand why they would always laugh when I would tell them about the things I had learned about them and their world. I continued my investigations and in the process I learned something about their concepts of sickness and health and about their ways of dealing with sickness. These understandings helped me to open many doors and, in the long run, to open my own eyes.

It all came to a head one day when Don Oswaldo, the watchman at the retreat house where I was living, asked me to go and to give the last rites to a nephew of his who was supposedly dying. Because the nephew was a robust young man who had broken a leg in a fall, I had no sense that he was in danger of death. The strangest part of all was that his uncle, Don Oswaldo, was one of the most respected native healers in the area. Obviously there was much more going on here than I could understand.

After a lot of discussion, Oswaldo and I came to an agreement that we would go together to visit the nephew. What was expected of me was that I would hear his confession, give him the holy oils, and let nature take its course. However, that is not what I did.

Applying what I had learned in my studies, when we reached the house I asked for an incense bowl and then I began "calling the spirits" in typical Aymara fashion, but with a twist. I called on the spirits by reciting the Canticle of Daniel (Dn 3:57–80) to put us into the presence of all of nature and God's creation. I then passed the incense bowl to Oswaldo so he could continue with his own invocations. He did. I then asked him to read the coca leaves to discover what the problem was and why such a healthy man was going to die from a broken leg. In due time what came to light was the fact that the nephew did not own any of his own land. He earned a living by working other peoples' land and by playing in a band. With his broken leg he could no longer work, and so he could not be a productive member of the community. By local values, he no longer had a right to live.

After a lot of discussion we decided to proceed with the next part of an Aymara healing rite: the pardon ceremony. In this ceremony the family of the sick man would have to pardon him for no longer being able to be productive and for becoming a burden on the community. The nephew, for his part, would have to pardon the family for being willing to let him die rather than accept the fact that he was going to need help and attention. The need for forgiveness was mutual and, thanks be to God, so was the will to do so. Everyone rose to the occasion. They really forgave one another and because there was no longer any need for him to die, he was healed.

During the course of the ceremony and its aftermath, the patient and I became good friends. Months after the ceremony he invited me to take a ride with him on Lake Titicaca. That afternoon he showed me any number of things that I didn't know about the lake, including its flora and fauna and its life in general. I knew that he was showing me something that I already knew—namely, that he knew much more about his world than I ever would.

When we arrived back at the shores of the lake he showed me how to find the springs of clean water with which to wash our feet. We both set out to wash, each in our own way. Then my friend looked at me and with a wry smile said, "You don't even know how to wash your feet right. Do I have to teach you everything?" And that's the way it was. He *did* have to teach me everything about the Aymara world, and he did so. For the rest of the time that we were together in the Altiplano he taught me about the life, the history, culture, language, social organization, and religious ideas and practices of the Aymaras. He did it from the point of view of the Aymaras themselves.

Instead of simply collecting data, I was learning the power of the community (a power that could give life or death). I learned a lot about the relationship between God and God's creation, and about the relationships between human beings and the rest of nature. I learned the power—and the necessity—of pardon and forgiveness, of mutuality, and of the values that are contained in and expressed by the myths that are told and are celebrated in the rites used to act out these values. I learned the depth of Aymara faith, which is an active and participative faith in God, in Jesus, and in the community. I learned to stop insisting that the Aymaras think and act like me before I would consider them to be true Christians. I learned to look at the world, God, and even myself with other eyes. Perhaps I would never be able to look at them with Aymara eyes, but I could at least use my "Aymaratized" eyes. Since then, whenever I spoke with the people about what I was learning, they no longer laughed at me. (FTM)

Theology

It is not everyone who says to me, "Lord, Lord," who will enter the kingdom of heaven, but the person who does the will of my Father in heaven. (Matthew 7:21)

When I lived in Venezuela, Victoria used to clean our house in Barinas every Tuesday morning. For twenty-six years she had been caring for a brain-damaged daughter. The child could not hear, see, or speak, but she smiled whenever the mother picked her up and held her. No other child had ever survived so long with that condition, and there is no doubt that it was the mother's love that permitted such a long life. Victoria had never studied theology, but some of her reflections made a profound impression on me.

The small group had gathered, as it did every Monday evening, for Bible reflection. This particular evening the text was from Matthew 12, with the words of Jesus concerning sins against the Spirit. Because the leader that night had rather dominated the conversation, I posed the question to everyone, "What would be a sin against the Holy Spirit?" The leader droned on for nearly ten minutes, and I had no idea what his point was. In part to try to promote community sharing, I asked Victoria directly, "Victoria, what do you think a sin against the Holy Spirit would be?" while admitting secretly to myself that I could probably not answer that question myself. Without a moment's hesitation she replied, "I think that if my neighbor needs help and I refuse to provide that help, that would be a sin against the Holy Spirit." I thought to myself that we should have this woman teaching theology in our seminaries.

Victoria listened as two of her neighbors, neither of whom was Catholic, were discussing what happens to the soul after death. One believed that the soul hovered over the body for a short time and then went to its eternal reward. The other claimed that the soul went immediately to its eternal reward with no time wasted. Then they asked Victoria what Catholics believed about the soul. She replied, "I don't know anything about what happens to the soul after death. What I know is that if my neighbor needs help, I have to give that help." (JAH)

Some years ago I was getting a haircut in the district town of Maswa in Tanzania. When I told the barber that I was flying to the United States, he asked me about the topics that Americans talk about and even disagree on. I mentioned the controversy over whether God should be called Father and Mother, or only Father. The barber commented, "That's an easy question. We are children of God. To give birth to children you need a Father and a Mother. So God has to be both."

Fr. Joseph G. Healey, M.M.
(from Baltimore)
Tanzania and Kenya

Time

Brother Loren W. Beaudry, M.M., from St. Cloud, Minnesota, has worked in Kenya and in formation in the United States. He has recently returned to mission in Namibia.

In the African culture greetings are a very important part of the daily routine. For instance, in Kenya, when meeting another person on the streets or on the road, a person will say something like *Habari za asabuihi?* (How is your morning?), *Habari za nyumbani?* (How are things at home?), *Habari za watoto wako?* (How are your children?), or *Umelalaje?* (How did you sleep last night?). I would often forget this and begin the day immediately with business. The first thing I might say to one of the workers would be, "Did you see so and so yesterday about fixing the pipes?" or "Did you pay yesterday's bill?" Wisely, they replied simply, "Habari za asabuhi, Brother Loren?" (What is the news today, Brother Loren?). I was always very embarrassed to realize that I was thinking first about business; for them, relationships were much more important than business. (LWB)

"What's wrong, Sabina?" I asked, "Is there something I can do for you?" Sabina, my cook, a robust Asmat woman in the Indonesian village of Sawa-Er in West Papua, is usually verbose and straightforward, but this time she put her head down, shuffled her feet, and mumbled almost inaudibly, "Will you teach me to tell time?"

I was intrigued—the only clock in the village of which I was aware here in my house, and it rarely worked properly. "Why do you want to be able to tell time?" I asked. "So I can cook your meals at the proper time," she replied. "But, Sabina," I exclaimed, "you have *sago* on the table every morning just as the sun breaks over the trees. You have fish on the table when the sun is straight overhead. And you have more *sago* back on the table as the sun eases itself into the river. How could you possibly improve on that?"

She was insistent, however, and since it seemed important to her, I complied. My lessons went on for days. We would sit on the floor, with Sabina calling upon all the spirits she could muster to help her concentrate. Beads of sweat would break out on her forehead. Her lips moved silently, telegraphing the struggle going on inside her head, but she just couldn't wrap her mind around the confounded concept.

I failed miserably as a teacher, but in truth I was secretly delighted that I had not corrupted her. There is something reassuring in that there are still some people on this good earth unconquered by the ubiquitous clock.

Fr. Vincent P. Cole, M.M.
(from Detroit, Michigan)
Indonesia

Tolerance

Rev. John C. Barth, M.M., from Buffalo, New York, has worked with the blind and with HIV/AIDS victims in Cambodia. Elected to the General Council of Maryknoll in 2002, he has now returned to Cambodia.

Tolerance. The people of Cambodia and Vietnam taught me about tolerance. After losing so much thirty years ago when U.S. war planes wiped their villages off the surface of the earth, today these fine people carry no grudges against me as an American. Every time I see the black MIA flag flying in this country, beneath our own Stars and Stripes, I think of the hundreds of thousands of Vietnamese and Cambodian and Laotian people who lost their lives and of the many who left this world without a trace—not unlike the innocent victims of 9/11.

On my occasional trips to Vietnam in the 1990s, I was reluctant at first to tell people I was an American, but soon I discovered, to my great surprise, that most Vietnamese still admire and respect Americans, even if they don't like what the American government did to their country. They are able to make the distinction between a people and their government. I feel welcome in South East Asia as an American. I learned tolerance and forgiveness from the people to whom I was sent as a missioner priest—to teach tolerance and forgiveness. (JCB)

Catching up on news—Vietnam

Tragedy

Paul Bork, from Buffalo, New York, is director of the Maryknoll Promotion House in Buffalo, New York. Once a Maryknoll seminarian, Paul left Maryknoll to work with the health commission in Buffalo. He is now married and the father of two daughters. Paul wrote the following article for the October 2005 issue of *Maryknoll Magazine*.

A former "lost boy of the Sudan" has said, "I believe that God has led me here." Faith, believes Samwel Majok Kuach, has led him on a fifteen-year journey from his village in southern Sudan to Ethiopia, then to Kenya, and finally over six thousand miles from eastern Africa to the United States.

Now twenty-eight and settled with newly found relatives in Syracuse, New York, Samwel works in a factory while studying for his high school equivalency diploma. He still vividly remembers his life as a refugee. When the army raided his village during Sudan's fierce civil war, nine-year-old Samwel joined a group of eight hundred homeless youth, all separated from their families and traveling together. For three months they trekked across the desert. Six hundred of them survived to arrive at a refugee camp in Ethiopia. They became known as the "lost boys of Sudan." Three years later they were forced to flee again, and Samwel ended up in Kakama, a refugee camp in Kenya. Under the auspices of the Migration and Refugee Services Office of the U.S. Conference of Catholic Bishops, Samwel finally arrived in Seattle at age twenty-four.

Maryknoll Father John Barth and Brother Tim Raible met him there. Former Maryknoll lay missioner Kip Hargrave, now director of resettlement for Catholic Charities in Syracuse, helped Samwel settle in that city in north central New York. Recently Samwel began a new phase of his journey.

He has participated in several vocation discernment retreats for young men considering a missionary vocation at the Maryknoll center in New York. "My Maryknoll friends and others who helped have been a blessing," he says. "Now I hope to be a blessing for others." (PB)

Truth in Wine—*In Vino Veritas*

The word of God is something alive and active: it cuts
more incisively than any two-edged sword: it can seek out
the place where soul is divided from spirit, or joints from
marrow; it can pass judgment on secret emotions and
thoughts. (Hebrews 4:12)

One of the reasons I am writing this book stems from an incident that happened both to me and for me many years ago. When I had been ordained about six months, the pastor of our parish, Fr. Dan Daly, had become so ill with a bleeding ulcer that everyone thought, at seventy-five years of age, he would not recover. However, recover he did, and a week after his return to the parish, the Mens' Club organized a dinner and testimonial for him at a local restaurant. On the way to the event I realized that the emcee would ask me to say a few words and so I tried to remember some funny experiences that would illustrate what a great man Fr. Daly was. Sure enough, they called on me to speak, and I gave my little testimonial using more humor than would be appropriate for a Sunday sermon.

After the dinner, as people milled around, one of the parishioners approached me. He had a martini in his left hand, and judging from his unsteady gait, he probably had more than one under his belt when he put out his right hand to shake mine. He said, "That was a great speech, Father, you were talking right from here." With that he jabbed his right index finger into my chest. Needless to say, I was very flattered. However, the sense of elation turned into deflation when he added, "Why don't you preach that way on Sunday?"

I am grateful that the good Lord helped me not to respond in anger, which was my first reaction. Instead the expression *in vino veritas* came to mind. In time, I was grateful to him because he had done me a great favor. (JAH)

Epilogue

Every teacher carries out his or her duty with intentionality. The goal is to teach, to communicate some information, or to guide toward some formation. When the poor teach, they have no idea at all that they are giving any lessons. They are just living their lives. That is a great part of the beauty of what they do.

Their wisdom comes in part from their lack of formal education. Just as those who have lost their sight develop their senses of touch and hearing more than the rest of us, so the poor, those who have not had the benefit of an education, develop incredible talents of observation and insight.

Maria cooked for our team. It was only when I left her a note one day that I discovered that she could not read or write. Yet she was a genius in the kitchen. She never measured when she made a cake but just seemed to throw the ingredients together willy-nilly. You could arrive at any hour and with any number of extra guests, and she would never bat an eye.

One day a family of friends stopped by, and among the visitors was a sixteen-year-old girl. When I introduced my friends to Maria, she said to the sixteen year old, "Oh, when are you expecting?" The young woman became angry and, very indignant, insisted that she was not pregnant. As one might imagine, that was a very tense moment for everyone, but we moved into the living room and soon Maria served tea. After the guests left, I asked Maria why she had said that and she replied, "Father, that girl is pregnant." I could not imagine scolding Maria, but I suggested that she be more careful in the future because the young lady should know whether she was with child or not.

Four months later we received word that the young woman in question had given birth. I informed Maria and apologized at the same time. Then I asked her how she knew the girl was pregnant. She said, "When a woman is with child after five months, if you look at her throat, you can see the baby's heart beat next to the mother's." I have asked any number of obstetricians about that phenomenon and only found one who had even heard of it. He said, "I have heard of people who can detect that, but I've never been able to."

I never wished illiteracy for Maria, or for anyone else, but I envied the power and the depth of her perceptions. Neither would I ever wish poverty on anyone, but those who cannot depend on wealth, power, education, or political influence have learned to depend on the Lord, and that is the basis of faith.

The poor have been gifted in many ways, and not the least is their perception of the gospel message and their ability to live it. As one bishop in Venezuela delighted in reminding the missioners who arrived on his shores, "History did not begin when your boat docked here." In other words, because the Holy Spirit was alive and moving long before our arrival, it is incumbent on us as missionarers to discover how and where the Spirit is working in the lands to which we go.

In *Becoming Local Church*, Fr. James H. Kroeger writes:

The Holy Spirit continually penetrates the concrete lives and histories of people from within and offers them a real mutual participation in the paschal mystery. Yes, for the Christian it will certainly be explicitly Christological. However, the identical experience, although often in an inchoate form, is continually available to all peoples—whatever their particular religious affiliation. (p. 123)

The basis for this belief is found in the document *Gaudium et Spes (The Pastoral Constitution on the Church in the Modern*

World) of the Second Vatican Council: "We must hold that the Holy Spirit offers to all the possibility of being made partners, in a way known to God, in the Paschal Mystery" (no. 22). It is, therefore, the task of the missioner and the pastoral agent not only to live the Paschal Mystery in his or her own life but also to discover it in the other. The preacher should listen to the congregation—their hopes, fears, and struggles. The eucharistic minister must discover and listen to Christ in the sick and the imprisoned.

The first step in a life of faith is a sense of awe and wonder. Whether you view the universe through a telescope and look into expanding space, wondering how and where it expands, or whether you look into the most powerful microscope and get a glimpse of the mighty atom, a source of incredible power, you stand in profound admiration of all creation. One of the great joys and rewards of a missioner is to have learned the wisdom of God from the little ones. (JAH)

A poor but faithful family—Myanmar

Resources from Orbis Books

About the World of Mission

Patrick J. Brennan, *The Mission Driven Parish* (2007): a prophetic call to renew the Catholic Church in the United States from the bottom up.

Roger P. Schroeder, *What Is the Mission of the Church? A Guide for Catholics* (2008): an accessible guide to the "who, what, where, and why" of mission and its meaning for the local and universal church.

Africa

Donald H. Dunson, *Child, Soldier, Victim: The Loss of Innocence in Uganda* (2008): the story of former child soldiers in northern Uganda.

Joseph G. Healey, M.M., *Once Upon a Time in Africa: Stories of Wisdom and Joy* (2004).

James Martin, S.J., *This Our Exile: A Spiritual Journal with the Refugees of East Africa* (1999).

A. E. Orobator, S.J., *Theology Brewed in an African Pot* (2008): an introduction to Christian doctrine from an African perspective.

Miriam Therese Winter, *The Singer and the Song* (1999): working with refugees in Ethiopia and Cambodia.

Asia

John Dear, ed., *Mohandas Gandhi: Essential Writings* (2002).

Thomas A. Forsthoefel, ed., *The Dalai Lama: Essential Writings* (2008).

James H. Kroeger, M.M., *Once Upon a Time in Asia: Stories of Harmony and Peace* (2006).

Jean Maalouf, *Mother Teresa: Essential Writings* (2001).

Bob McCahill, *Dialogue of Life: A Christian among Allah's Poor* (1996): a Christian living among poor Muslims in Bangladesh.

Latin America

Ana Carrigan, *Salvadoran Witness: The Life and Calling of Jean Donovan* (2005): the story of one of the four American churchwomen slain in El Salvador.

Marie Dennis, Renny Golden, and Scott Wright, eds., *Oscar Romero: Reflections on His Life and Writings* (2000).

Roseanne Murphy, S.N.D., *Martyr of the Amazon: The Life of Sister Dorothy Stang* (2007).

General

Donald H. Dunson, *No Room at the Table: Earth's Most Vulnerable Children* (2007): the stories of issues affecting the world's children: sexual exploitation, child labor, homelessness, hunger, and poverty.

Robert Ellsberg, ed., *Charles de Foucauld: Writings* (1991): the story of a monastic living among the Muslim poor of Algeria.

Mark Kramer, *Dispossessed: Life in Our World's Urban Slums* (2006): stories of the slums of Manila, Nairobi, Mexico City, Bangkok, and Cairo.

Michael Leach and Susan Perry, eds., *A Maryknoll Book of Prayer* (2003): prayers from Maryknollers around the world.

These and other books available from Orbis Books are listed at www.orbisbooks.com.